MW01274781

Larry's Party

A MUSICAL
BASED ON THE NOVEL BY
CAROL SHIELDS

BOOK AND LYRICS
Richard Ouzounian

MUSIC
Marek Norman

McArthur & Company
Toronto

Canadian Cataloguing in Publication Data

Ouzounian, Richard, 1950 –
  Larry's Party : the musical

Includes 4 songsheets.
ISBN 1-55278-193-3

I. Norman, Marek. II. Shields, Carol, 1935 –   . Larry's party.
III. Title.

PS8579.U96L37 2001   C812'.54   C00-933163-8
PR9199.3.O99L37 2001

Composition and Design by *Michael P. Callaghan*
Typeset at *Moons of Jupiter, Inc.* (Toronto)
Cover and Illustration Design by *Doowah Design Inc.*
Printed in Canada by *Transcontinental Printing Inc.*

McArthur & Company
322 King Street West, Suite 402
Toronto, ON, M5V 1J2

10 9 8 7 6 5 4 3 2 1

The publisher wishes to acknowledge the financial support of the
Government of Canada through the Book Publishing Industry
Development Program (BPIDP) for our publishing activities.
The publisher further wishes to acknowledge the financial support
of the Ontario Arts Council for our publishing program.

This one is for Pamela.

*"The woman that you marry
is part of you for life."*

NOTES ON *LARRY'S PARTY*

"Where you start from, there you end," Carol Shields tells us on the final page of *Larry's Party*.

But where did the musical version of her book actually start? With a phone call, of course, like most theatrical projects.

Morley Walker of the *Winnipeg Free Press* called me out of the blue one day in the summer of 1997 to ask if I would be interested in reviewing Carol Shields' new novel, *Larry's Party*, for his paper.

I immediately said yes, as I was a huge fan of Carol's work, and had the pleasure of knowing her slightly from our mutual years in Winnipeg during the early '80s.

But then I asked Morley why he had chosen me. "You seem a lot like Larry to me," was his answer. "You're the same age, lived in Winnipeg at the same time, got married at the same time, lots of things."

I read the book and gave it a glowing review. Fade out.

Fade in on an April night the next year, 1998. My long-time collaborator Marek Norman and I were driving home from a show at Toronto's Canadian Stage Theatre.

At that time, we had productions of our *Dracula* scheduled for Halifax that fall, and our *Emily* in Charlottetown the following summer. "Wouldn't it be nice if we could drive home from rehearsal in ten minutes like this," offered Marek, "instead of always having to go out of town?"

I agreed, and we both commented that Canadian Stage had such a high standard of production that it would be a pleasure to do a show there. And Martin Bragg had just taken over as Artistic Producer, so the time was ripe to hit him with a fresh idea.

I've known Marty for twenty years, and he likes work that is Canadian, and work that is popular . . . ideally both at the same time. What better way to combine them than in an adaptation of a popular Canadian novel? And what was more popular at that time than Carol Shields' new best-seller, *Larry's Party*?

Marek had loved the book, and you already know how I felt about it. I went home that night, picked it up again, and it fell open by chance to a passage near the end: "And we will go round and around. Watching where we're going. Where we've been."

That almost read like a song lyric to me.

We were halfway home. The next day I set about contacting Carol. It wasn't hard. A quick search of the e-mail directory at the University of Winnipeg where she was then Chancellor gave me what I needed.

I sent out a cheerful and cheeky request for the rights to turn *Larry's Party* into a musical.

Forty-five minutes later Carol's answer appeared on my screen:

"Richard, I never thought of it that way, but you know more about musicals than I do, so go ahead with my blessing."

I picked up the phone and called Marty Bragg. After some preliminary congratulatory chat, I cut to the chase.

"Marty, do you know *Larry's Party*?"

"Love it. On the top of my to-do list. Want to get the rights to turn it into a play."

"Too late, Marty, I've got them. And it's going to be a musical."

"Then you better write it for us."

"That was the idea."

Done like dinner, less than twenty-four hours after the idea first hit.

Then came the hard part, writing it. I began by visiting Carol in Winnipeg, and talking to her about Larry and his book. "Don't make him a buffoon," she pleaded. "I love Larry." I loved him too — so of course I agreed.

By the end of November, 1999, we had finished a first draft, and had done a presentation for Canadian Stage and several other theatres. The result was immediate and positive.

Early in 2000, we had a three-city Canadian tour lined up and the brilliant Robin Phillips set to direct an impeccable cast led by my friend and colleague of thirty years, the uniquely wonderful Brent Carver.

Months of rewriting followed, under the watchful eyes of Robin and of Katherine Kaszas of Canadian Stage's New Play Development Program. And then, before I knew it, we were into rehearsal, which is proving to be a thrilling process as I write these words.

Turning the story of Larry Weller, master maze-maker, into a musical has been a unique journey. And it all began with a book and a phone call.

Welcome to Larry's Party. I'm so glad you're here.

— Richard Ouzounian
December, 2000

LARRY'S PARTY received its world premiere from the Canadian Stage Company at the Bluma Appel Theatre in Toronto on January 11, 2001.

It was subsequently presented at the National Arts Centre in Ottawa, and the Manitoba Theatre Centre in Winnipeg.

CAST:
(in order of speaking)

LARRY   *Brent Carver*
DORRIE   *Susan Gilmour*
DOT, ERLEEN, MARCIA, ETC.   *Jane Johanson*
MIDGE, WAITRESS, ETC.   *Michelle Fisk*
RYAN, HECTOR, SAM, ETC.   *Mike Nadajewski*
STU, ARTHUR, BRUCE, GARTH, ETC.   *Gary Krawford*
CHARLOTTE, VIVIAN, SALLY, ETC.   *Barbara Barsky*
HERSH, JOHNNY, IAN, ETC.   *Jack Wetherall*
BETH, STEWARDESS, DOCTOR, ETC.   *Julain Molnar*

Director: Robin Phillips
Musical Director: Paul Sportelli
Set Design: Hashim Ali
Costume Design: Janice Lindsay
Lighting Design: Louise Guinand
Sound Design: John Lott
Orchestrator: Jim Pirie

Assistant Director: Anne Wootten
Assistant Musical Director: Neil Bartram
Stage Manager: Vince Berns
Assistant Stage Manager: Larry Copeland

Artistic Producer: Martin Bragg
Dramaturg: Katherine Kazsas

ACT I

Scene One

FIFTEEN MINUTES IN THE LIFE
OF LARRY WELLER

(We hear the soundscape of a party in progress. Eight people are together for a dinner party. We suddenly see a ninth: LARRY WELLER.)

LARRY:
> Look around the room,
> look at all the people.
> People that I know,
> people that I knew.
>
> Some of them I loved,
> some have even loved me.
> Some are here to stay,
> some are passing through.
>
> But they all
> are the pieces of my life,
> from the past,
> from today.
> Every one
> of the pieces of my life,
> takes me home,
> takes me home.

Something has happened in this room. It's almost as if there are two realities here, one suspended inside the other. And the air around the table, candlelit, soft, breaks up into shimmering bars of heat. A mirage? Perhaps. But here we are.

(DORRIE steps from the group to join LARRY.)

DORRIE:
Did you mean what you said at the table tonight? That you weren't really lost that time we were in Hampton Court?

LARRY:
Not exactly. I was lost, but I wanted to be lost.

DORRIE:
Why didn't you tell me?

LARRY:
I wasn't sure you'd understand.

DORRIE:
I would've understood. But I wouldn't have known how to tell you that I understood.

LARRY:
Was that our problem? That we didn't know enough words?

DORRIE:
Or what we were allowed to say.

LARRY:
We could have said anything. We should have learned.

DORRIE:
Tell me, Larry, do you still want to be lost?

LARRY:
No, not any more. I want . . .

DORRIE:
What?

LARRY:
To get myself . . . found.

(DORRIE and all the other guests seem to fade away, leaving LARRY alone.)

> Watching where we're going,
> wondering where we've gone.
> Half of life is knowing,
> the rest is moving on.
>
> After all the racing,
> funny, but it's true.
> Through the nights and the days,
> at the end of the maze is . . .

(We've gone back in time, we hear the sound of a distant lullaby. LARRY'S mother comes forward. Her name is DOT.)

DOT:
Smile, luv, smile for your mum. That's it.

We will go round and round again,
singing the songs our hearts have sung.

My Larry. I picked your name myself. I just thought it
sounded like a real boy's name. Like Jack. Now that's
another name I like. It's, you know, masculine. There's
nothing silly about it, but at the same time it isn't one
of your stuffed-shirt names. I wanted you to have a
middle name too, and John had a nice royal ring to it.
So there you are. Laurence John Weller. My Larry.

As we go round and round,
and round and round and round again.

(DOT drifts into the background, leaving LARRY to speak to us.)

LARRY:
I never really liked my first name much. Larry. Rhymes
with ordinary. And my middle name, John? A blank,
just occupying space. But my last name, Weller, that
I've learned to love. *(As if quoting from a reference book:)*
"One who lives within the sight and sound of running water, a water man, a well man, a custodian of
all that is clear, pure sustaining and everlastingly present."

*(The eight members of our ENSEMBLE move forward, and help
change the time and place we're in.)*

ENSEMBLE:
Fifteen minutes
in the life,
in the life of Larry Weller.

Ordinary fella,
quiet kinda guy.
Funny how they send him
where the air is high.

So send him up
where the sun is blazing.
Way, way up,
its amazing glow,

Sort of stuck
in the everyday world.
But today, world,
watch him go.

Fifteen minutes
in the life,
in the life of Larry Weller.

LARRY:
A cold April night like this.

ENSEMBLE:
Larry Weller.

LARRY:
Over twenty years ago.

ENSEMBLE:
Larry Weller.

(We're inside a coffee shop.)

MAN:
Shut the door, buddy.

WAITRESS:
Hey, Larry, the usual?

LARRY:
You bet.

> Nickels and dimes
> ring in my pocket,
> pieces of time
> ring in my head.
>
> Think of the girl
> waiting to meet me,
> music and light
> right up ahead.

WAITRESS:
Warm that up for you?

LARRY:
Warm enough in here already . . .

(LARRY takes his tweed jacket off and hangs it up.)

> It's so fine
> to be young
> and alive,
> and all new.
> It's all mine,
> it's all real,

and it's all
comin' true.
Oh, oh, oh, oh, oh.

I'm gonna be late. Dorrie'll *kill* me. *(To WAITRESS)*
Check!

    Nickels and dimes
    takin' me places,
    mountains to climb,
    cities to see.

(LARRY pays her, gives her a tip.)

    Think of it all
    startin' tomorrow.
    Look at the world
    wavin' at me.

(LARRY starts out. The WAITRESS stops him, and hands him the wrong tweed sports coat.)

WAITRESS:
You might need this . . . it's windy out there.

LARRY:
It's always windy out there.

(LARRY leaves the coffee shop and continues down the street.)

    Life is a song
    that you can't
    start singin'

till you learn all
of the rhymes.
They're here
in my pocket,
along with the
nickels and dimes.

Oh, oh, oh oh.
Oh, oh, oh oh . . .

Wait a minute! No nickels and dimes . . . no bus trans-
fers . . . this isn't my jacket! This one is . . . much nicer.
The lining. The buttons. Leather, the real thing. So
this is what Harris Tweed is *supposed* to feel like. How
was I supposed to know? I never knew anyone even
wore Harris Tweed anymore.

(*HECTOR, a clothing salesman, joins DOT at LARRY's side.*)

HECTOR:
Believe me, lady, that's value for money. It's a classic.

DOT:
It won't show the dirt.

HECTOR:
It'll never go out of style.

DOT:
I like this nubby-dubby cloth. It's smooth and rough
at the same time . . .

HECTOR:
Heavy, but also light.

DOT:
With these soft little hairs riding on top of the weave.

LARRY:
It's not very . . . dressy.

DOT:
Laurence John Weller, you are graduating from Red River College with your Floral Arts Diploma. I want something you'll get plenty of use out of.

HECTOR:
And this jacket! Not only could you wear it to work, but you could even wear it to a do at the Prime Minister's.

DOT:
Could you now?

HECTOR:
Absolutely.

(DOT and HECTOR drift back. LARRY's on the street again.)

LARRY:
I hated that old jacket, but this one, this one makes me feel different. Sure, I'm still just Larry Weller, I'm a floral designer, twenty-six years old, and I'm walking down Notre Dame Avenue in the city of Winnipeg in the country of Canada in the month of April in the year 1977. The wind is blowing, my heart is pounding, and all of a sudden I'm thinking. I'm thinking hard . . . about being hungry, about having sex with Dorrie later on tonight, about how great I feel in this

other guy's jacket and how the rest of my life is gonna be better and special.

(*A MAN chases after LARRY, waving his old tweed jacket.*)

MAN:
Hey buddy, buddy . . . wait up.

LARRY:
What is it?

MAN:
You took my jacket by mistake.

LARRY:
Oh . . . it's really nice.

MAN:
Don't I know it.

(*They exchange jackets, the MAN leaves. LARRY continues down the street.*)

LARRY:
Nickels and dimes
ring in my pocket,
pieces of time
ring in my head

Think of the girl
waitin' to meet me,
music and light
right up ahead,

right up ahead,
right up ahead!

(He spots DORRIE and runs into her arms.)

Dorrie . . . !

DORRIE:
I love you, Larry.

(END OF SCENE)

Scene Two

LARRY'S LOVE

(STU, LARRY's father, appears behind him.)

STU:
So. You in love with this girl? You in love with her?

LARRY:
What?

STU:
Love. You heard me.

LARRY:
I like her a lot.

STU:
But you're not in love?

LARRY:
I don't know.

STU:
You're twenty-six years old. I married your Mum when I was twenty-five.

LARRY:
Yeah. Twenty-six years old and the kid's still living at home.

STU:
Did I say there was anything wrong with that?

(STU disappears.)

DORRIE:
Larry? I said I love **you**.

LARRY:
I love you too, Dorrie.

DORRIE:
Then let's just fuck and fuck and fuck forever.

LARRY:
Do you have to say that? Can't you just say . . . "making love"?

DORRIE:
You say "fuck." You say it all the time.

LARRY:
No, I don't.

DORRIE:
Come off it. You're always saying "fuck this" and "fuck that."

LARRY:
Maybe. Maybe I do. But I don't mean it literally.

DORRIE:
What?

LARRY:
Not *literally*.

DORRIE:
Literalaly . . . another fucking college word!

LARRY:
I only went to *flower* college . . .

(LARRY finds himself at home with DOT and STU.)

DOT:
And that was an accident, love, a fluke. You'd only been out of school a few weeks . . . and you were just moping around the house, so I phoned Red River College one day and asked them to send me their brochure on the Furnace Repair course. I figure everyone in Winnipeg has a furnace, so they were a good thing to get into. But someone must have been sleeping at the switch, because they sent you a pamphlet from Floral Arts. Flowers instead of Furnaces.

STU:
Flowers.

LARRY:
Sorry, Dad.

DOT:

He came to your graduation, but he didn't know where to look. Even when Mrs. Starr presented you with the Rose Wreath for having the top point average, he just sat there with his chin scraping the floor.

(VIVIAN, 40ish and pleasant, is at a counter arranging flowers.)

VIVIAN:

Then you came to work for us at Flowerfolks, and boy, were you a breath of fresh air. I don't know, Larry, maybe I've been here too long, but I used to think that if I had to wire one more chrysanthemum stem, I was gonna scream. But it's all fresh to you, all new, all special.

LARRY:

I like it, Vivian. I like working with flowers. I feel as though I'm part of something living, something growing. I like that.

VIVIAN:

Well, that centrepiece you did for the mayor's banquet last October was a triumph! The sprays of wheat, the eucalyptus branches . . . and the baby orchids. What an inspired touch! Brilliant.

LARRY:

Thanks, Vivian.

VIVIAN *(handing him a bouquet)***:**

Here, Larry, for you and Dorrie, with love from all of us here at Flowerfolks.

(A wedding procession begins forming. DORRIE is the bride.)

MINISTER:
It's Friday afternoon, March 8, 1978.

HERSH:
I've got the ring. That's the best man's job. To hold the ring till you ask for it. I've got it right here.

LARRY:
Thanks, Hersh.

HERSH:
Best friend, best man. I like the way that works out.

DOT:
Look at him, Stu. Isn't he handsome?

STU:
Nice haircut. Nice and short.

DOT:
That's Dorrie's influence. More power to her . . .

LARRY AND DORRIE:
It's so fine
to be young
and in love
and with you.
It's all mine,
it's all real,
and it's all
comin' true.

(We hear the sound of an airplane and the wedding group become passengers.)

STEWARDESS:
Please fasten your seatbelts . . . Air Canada Flight 514, non-stop service from Winnipeg to London, England, is about to depart . . . and we thought you'd like to know we've got a brand-new married couple aboard our flight today. How about a round of applause, everyone, for Mr. and Mrs. Larry Weller of Winnipeg, Manitoba. *(She pins a corsage on DORRIE.)*

DORRIE:
Ohh! This is fabulous! How did you know? Baby roses, I love baby roses, and look, they match my outfit. It's perfect.

LARRY:
It's a pretty outfit, Dorrie.

DORRIE:
It's a polyester-blend. It's not supposed to wrinkle. But, like a dope, I didn't bring along some spot lifter. You see that? By the time we get to England, that'll be permanently set. *(She yawns.)* They put dye in airplane food to make it look more appetizing. Really. *(Another yawn.)* They do. One of the guys at work told me all about it . . . *(She's asleep.)*

LARRY:
I'm your husband now, Dorrie. Your husband. And I'll take care of you. I'll take care of us. I'll be good and solid and quiet and true. Just like my Dad . . .

STEWARDESS:
We're beginning our descent into London's Heathrow Airport. Make sure that your seat belts are securely fastened, your tray-tables are in an upright position, and all your personal belongings are safely stored under the seat in front of you . . .

LARRY:
Look, Dorrie, it's so green. I never thought it would be this green. So many gardens. So many hedges, look at them, running through the countryside like the veins in my arm, twisting into patterns, into mazes, into puzzles that we have to solve. Everything is growing. Everything is full of life. Everything is just beginning. For you. For me. For us.

(Our airplane passengers turn into a tour group, led by ARTHUR — brisk and British.)

ARTHUR:
Welcome to Sunbrite Tours, ladies and gents . . . 12 days by bus . . . from the Pennines down to Land's End . . . all of England will be yours, thanks to your obedient servant, Arthur Edwards. Come along . . .

DORRIE:
Oh Larry, look at all the rest of them! Everyone's so old. Everyone's old and fat except for us. I'll bet we're the only ones who screw all night. Or screw at all.

LARRY:
Probably.

DORRIE:
Notice I said screw and not fuck.

LARRY:
Congratulations.

DORRIE:
I'm a married woman now. Respectable.

LARRY:
Ha.

DORRIE:
Ha yourself.

ARTHUR:
Hurry up, you honeymooners!

ENSEMBLE:
You honeymooners!

ARTHUR:
Come on, Mr. Weller . . . and I'll show you some more of those hedges you find so fascinating. Your wife seems a bit tetchy . . .

LARRY:
We're going to have a baby. My wife, I mean. We were going to wait and get married in June. But this happened . . . so here we are. March.

ARTHUR:
Look at the time! Hurry along, Mr. Weller.

DORRIE *(who's been listening)*:
Why? Why would you go and tell a total stranger about us?

LARRY:
It just came out. We were talking and it slipped out.

DORRIE:
We're the lovey-dovey honeymooners, for God's sake, only now the little bride person is pregnant.

LARRY:
No one even thinks like that anymore.

DORRIE:
Oh yeah? What about your mother and father? They think like that.

LARRY:
How do you know what they think?

DORRIE:
They think no one's good enough for their precious little Larry, especially girls dumb enough to go and get themselves preggo.

LARRY:
They'll get used to it

DORRIE:
Like it's my fault. Like you didn't have one little thing to do with it, right? I can just see your dad looking at me. That look of his, oh boy. Like don't I have any brains? Like why wasn't I on the pill?

LARRY:
We'll tell them as soon as we get back. It'll take them a day or two, that's all. Then they'll get used to it.

DORRIE:
And what about you? When are you going to get used to it?

LARRY:
I am used to it.

DORRIE:
Oh yeah, sure. I'm like sitting there on the bus, day after day, thinking up names. Girls' names, boys' names. That's what's in my head. I like Victoria for a girl. For a boy I like Troy. Those kinds of thoughts. And you're jumping up and down looking at bushes. That's all you care about. Goddamn fucking bushes.

(The tour bus transforms into a garden maze.)

ARTHUR:
>Welcome to Hampton Garden
>the highlight of our days.
>stick close to me
>and you will see
>the most amazing maze.
>At Hampton Court,
>the greatest sport
>was leading folks astray.
>So welcome to Hampton Garden,
>it's time to find the way . . .

Before you, ladies and gents, is the oldest surviving hedge maze in England.

LARRY:
A what?

ARTHUR:
A hedge maze, Mr. Weller, made of yew branches. Trapezoid in shape, 222 by 82 feet, designed in 1690 to frustrate and delight the court of William and Mary, and still here in 1978 to do the same to the patrons of Sunbrite Tours. Are we ready?

(ARTHUR leads them into the maze.)

We will go round and round again,
follow along, and come with me.

Turn left,
right, right,
left, left, left, left.
That's how you take the chance, sir,
that's how you learn the answer,
that's how you get the key.

Then right,
right, right,
right, right, left, left;
and if you're persevering,
the voices you keep hearing
will bring you home and free.
So come along with me . . .

(The group moves ahead, leaving LARRY alone.)

LARRY:

Watching where I'm going,
wondering where I've gone.
Never really knowing
but I keep moving on.

After all the racing,
who knows what I'll see?
Through the nights and the days,
at the end of the maze
is me . . .

I'm lost,
so lost
totally lost
a sort of sweet surrender.
Stop playing the pretender,
what am I waiting for?

I'm lost,
more lost,
utterly lost:
beyond all comprehension,
and every good intention
can't lead me back once more
to where I was before . . .

Lost my chance
lost my place,
lost in time
lost in space.

(LARRY suddenly sees the centre of the maze and finds his way there.)

Through the twisting
and the turning
finally learning
where to go.

Past the terror
and the doubting
till I'm shouting
what I know.

There's a place
where I'm protected,

there's a spot
where I can stay.
I'm prepared to take that chance, sir,
I believe I'll learn the answer.
I will find the way,
I will find the way!

(END OF SCENE)

Scene Three

LARRY'S FOLKS

(The maze becomes the garden of LARRY's house.)

HERSH:
I'm Hersh. Well, you see, my name's Bill Hershel, but everybody calls me Hersh. I've been Larry's best friend since we were kids. When he first started seeing Dorrie, we drifted apart a bit. That's only natural. Same thing happened when I married Heather. But, funny, now that we're both old married guys, we spend more time together. I help him with his house. He bought a place over on Lipton Street, a handyman special, just five rooms and a glassed-in porch. Lots of stuff needs fixing . . .

(DORRIE enters, pushing RYAN in his stroller.)

DORRIE:
You've got to lay new tiles in the kitchen, then the bathroom fixtures need replacing, and maybe some ceiling insulation before winter comes along.

HERSH:
But most of the time, he's working in his yard. That's where he is today. August 17, 1980 . . . his thirtieth birthday.

DORRIE:

See, Ryan? I told you. Daddy's out here with his bushes.

LARRY:

They're shrubs.

DORRIE:

You've got shrub mania. You want to be the shrub king of the universe.

LARRY:

And what if I do? What if I build a maze that people will come from all over the world to see? Isn't everybody allowed one minute of fame in their lives?

DORRIE:

Why do you need fame, anyway? You've got a wife, a kid, a house, a job. That's it, Larry. That's your life. Get used to it.

LARRY:

How's Ryan?

DORRIE:

He's asleep. Don't wake him. . . . Come on, let's go to your folks and get it over with. Bet Dot's been slaving all day for her Larry. Bet we're to going have to eat a hot dinner, gravy and all, at the bitch end of a sizzling day. Jesus . . .

(DORRIE, LARRY and RYAN have traveled to DOT and STU's.)

DOT:
Larry, my love . . . happy birthday!

STU:
Best of the day.

DOT:
Hello Dorrie.

DORRIE:
Dot. Stu.

LARRY:
Where's Midge?

DOT:
She said she'd be here.

DORRIE:
Your sister's never been on time in her life.

LARRY:
Give her a break, Dorrie. Give us all a break.

STU:
How's baby Ryan?

DORRIE:
He's asleep. Don't . . .

LARRY:
. . . wake him.

DOT:

I've made all your favourites. Lancashire Hot Pot.

DORRIE:

Yum.

LARRY:

Sounds great, Mum.

DOT:

And Lemon Meringue Pie. It's in the fridge. Just to be safe. . . . Now where's my Ryan, my little Rye-Krisp, my little Ribena, my mister Man, my Noodle-Doodle . . .

(LARRY steps out of time to look at DOT.)

LARRY:

My mother. My sad soft mother. A housewife, a maker of custard sauce, a knitter of scarves, a fervent keeper of baby pictures and family scrapbooks. But her real work is sorrowing, remembering, absorbing her grievous history, trying to go forward when all this heaviness lies inside. One ancient mistake, one hour gone wrong, and now she pays and pays . . .

(Now DOT steps out of time to speak to us.)

DOT:

I was twenty-five years old and married to young Stu Weller who worked as an upholsterer for British Railways up north in Bolton. Our little Midge had just taken her first steps. I was pregnant with my Larry. And I was very happy. I had a tiny garden where I grew lettuce, radishes, carrots, and a wavy row of runner beans. I stewed the beans and preserved them in sealed jars, twelve pints in all, blue-green in colour, gleaming from the pantry shelf. One Sunday, Mum and Dad Weller came to dinner, and I served roast beef and mash and gravy and a choice of Brussels sprouts . . . or the beans. Only Mum Weller helped herself to the beans, and rather generously, too. After we ate, Stu and his Dad put Midge in her pram and took her for a walk. Then, all of a sudden, Mum Weller told me she was having trouble swallowing. Then she groaned and fell forward with a crash onto the hearth rug. Her head was twisted to one side, and her face was purple. I thought it was a heart attack, but no, it turned out to be severe type C botulism. They said it was my beans . . . the same beans that had been standing in their pretty glass jars for the last two months, as purely green and sweet as innocence itself.

STU:
Dot, isn't it time to eat yet?

DOT:
Pick up your forks . . .

LARRY:
Aren't we going to wait for Midge?

(MIDGE barges in, 30ish, hyper, dumps a package of bakery buns on the table and dives right in.)

MIDGE:
Sorry, sorry, sorry everyone. I've been away all weekend at an and anger workshop in Gimli. Two hundred women showed up. If you signed up early, you

got ten percent off, but I only heard about it on Friday afternoon. So I knocked off work early, said I had a headache, packed up the car and hit the road. Just a spur of the moment thing. There was an anger workshop leader up from the States. Yeah really. That's her specialty. What a woman! Grey hair down to her waist, barefoot, got a PhD in something or other, travels all over the place, writes books, gives lectures, TV talk shows, Phil Donahue, all that kind of stuff. Holler it out. That's what she told us. Scream, yell, weep till you pee, hang on to each other. Tell your story, then bury it. That's just what we did. We gathered on the beach early this morning just as the sun was coming up over the horizon of Lake Winnipeg, two hundred shouting, half-clothed women. And then each of us threw into the water a symbolic pebble, our compacted rage, our flinty little burden of hoarded injustice. Oh God, it was beautiful! The peace, the stillness, the light on the water . . . and then the fucking traffic coming home . . . it was a nightmare.

DORRIE:
What are all you chicks so angry about?

MIDGE:
Lots of things. Lousy men, lousy jobs, lousy lives. Hey, call me strange, but I'm still angry about the fact that my husband turned out to be gay . . .

DOT:
Poor Paul. I knew there was something funny-bunny about him from day one.

MIDGE:
But I'm over that now. We all have to face the past and bury it.

STU:
Easier said than done.

DOT:
No . . .

STU:
We used to be so happy, back in England. Me and Dot, and baby Midge . . .

MIDGE:
> Larry's pappy,
> such a happy chappy,
> loves his tiny tot.
>
> Hugs his missus,
> covers her with kisses.
> She's his darling Dot.
>
> Life's so cheery,
> never teary, dearie.
> Sun is shining bright.

STU:
> But all of that can change in a single night.

MIDGE:
> You want to see how fate intervenes?
> Try Dot's Amazing Beans . . .

STU AND MIDGE:
Beans, beans,
Dot's amazing beans.

MIDGE:
Green as men from Mars.

STU:
Little men from Mars.

MIDGE:
Just one catch:

MIDGE AND STU:
A batch of botulism
is lurking in the jars.
Take one bite,

MIDGE:
you're out like a light,

STU AND MIDGE:
then you're pushing up the sod.
Oh, beans, beans,
Dot's amazing beans.
It's one way to meet your God.

(The rest of the ENSEMBLE enter and help tell the story.)

MEN:
Dot's good lookin'.
Not so good at cooking.
Once she burned the tea.

WOMEN:
She keeps trying,
frying and then crying.

ENSEMBLE:
Lord, what misery!

This beginner
planned a Sunday dinner

WOMEN:
for her mum-in-law.

STU:
A culinary mess like you never saw.

MIDGE AND STU:
So if you're hopin' for haute cuisines,

ENSEMBLE:
try Dot's . . .

(MOTHER WELLER keels over dead.)

ENSEMBLE:
Beans, beans,
Dot's amazing beans.
Green as men from Mars.

Just one catch:
a batch of botulism
is lurking in the jars.

Take one bite,
you're out like a light,
then you're pushing up the sod.

Oh, beans, beans,
Dot's amazing beans.
It's one way to meet your . . .

STU, MIDGE AND DOT:
God deliver us from all the past, we beg:

ENSEMBLE:
it's time to start
a brand new life again
in Winnipeg with . . .

Beans, beans,
Dot's amazing beans.
Green as men from Mars.

WOMEN:
(little men from Mars!)

ENSEMBLE:
Just one catch:
a batch of botulism
is lurking in the jars.

Take one bite,
you're out like a light,
then you're pushing up the sod.

Oh, beans, beans,
Dot's amazing beans.
It's one way to meet your
it's one way to meet your
it's one way to meet your God.

(END OF SCENE)

Scene Four

LARRY'S WORK

(VIVIAN and LARRY are working at the flower shop.)

VIVIAN:
It's amazing, isn't it? Seventy-four percent of the nuts that a squirrel hides never get found. Well, I've been hiding nuts too. Remembering people's names, following up after weddings, sending those little anniversary reminders. And where has it got me?

LARRY:
I thought you loved it here.

VIVIAN:
I did. But I just couldn't wear this smock any more. I'm thirty-eight years old, Larry. If I wanted to be Little Bo-Peep, I'd go work at Disneyland.

LARRY:
I just can't imagine this place without you.

VIVIAN:
Try. You're the manager now. I told the head office you were ready to be in charge.

LARRY:
I can't believe it. I never thought . . .

VIVIAN:

Remember those squirrels? You've been burying your nuts all along — nothing personal, pal — and now it's time to go find a few. You deserve it, Larry. You'll be a great boss. Hey, what gives? You're supposed to be looking happy. You're going up the ladder, my laddie-boy . . .

(STU is at his workbench.)

STU:

For thirty years now, I've worked as an upholsterer for a custom-coach company in south Winnipeg. I love my job. My hands understand the secrets of foam and spring and frame. Some of North America's biggest and brightest names in the entertainment industry have bought customized vehicles from us. One country-western singer ordered a model with a bathroom door that dropped open, bingo, to reveal a hot tub where the luggage compartment usually goes. A cool half-million dollars for that package. That's my work. Work. That's what turns the gears of life . . .

(DORRIE enters, pushing RYAN in the stroller.)

DORRIE:

Before Larry and I got married, I was a clerk/receptionist in the parts division of Manitoba Motors. The pay wasn't great, but the customers loved me, 'cause I always sympathized with them over the size of their repair bills. They appreciated that. They nicknamed me Dorable. . . . After Ryan was born, I stayed home for three months . . .

(She leaves the stroller.)

But then I decided to go back to work, and they put me out on the sales floor. First thing I did was buy two perky little suits. A soft grey wool flannel and a nice brisk blue hound's-tooth check. Professional apparel. You see, times have changed. Women are out there buying their own vehicles, and they value the judgment of other women. You see, I can talk about transmission and power brakes, but I can also be deeply sympathetic to colour and upholstery combinations. Last April, I was top salesperson in the whole city. and I got a plaque with my name engraved on it, and a weekend for two at Hecla Island. Then I went straight out and bought a third suit, a raspberry linen blend, nice for summer, and a pair of high-heel sandals.

LARRY:
Congratulations.

DORRIE:
But I'm going to quit as soon as we've got enough money in the bank . . . enough to buy a place like we saw last weekend in Linden Woods . . . the one with the spiral staircase with the wrought-iron railing. Oh Larry, if we could just live in a house like that, I'd never work another day in my life.

LARRY:
I don't want to move.

DORRIE:
You just don't want to leave your crazy yard. You and your maze craze. Do you remember that day you

got lost at Hampton Court? . . . I've got news for you
. . . you're still lost.

(DORRIE storms out, leaving LARRY alone with RYAN.)

LARRY:
How you doin', Mister Man? Mister Ryan, Mister Rye-
Krisp, Mister Ribena . . . don't worry about your
Daddy. He'll be fine . . .

> I'm a part of you now,
> you're a part of me.
> Pieces of a puzzle
> no one else can see.
>
> Petals of a flower,
> ripples on a stream.
> Shadows in the twilight,
> voices in a dream.
>
> Who could understand it?
> Who would want to try?
> Let me hold the moment
> as it hurries by.
>
> Pieces of a puzzle
> no one else can see.
> I'm a part of you now
> you're a part of me.
>
> There's a thread
> that ties a father to his son,
> strong as steel,
> thin as air.

And I know
that now your life has just begun
in my arms
in my care.

Petals of a flower,
ripples on a stream.
Shadows in the twilight,
voices in a dream.

Pieces of a puzzle
no one else can see.
I'm a part of you now,
you're a part of me.

Yes, I'm a part of you now,
and you're a part of me.

(END OF SCENE)

Scene Five

LARRY'S WORDS

ENSEMBLE:
We will go round and round again . . .

DORRIE:
I'm going shopping . . . not that there's anything you'd want to buy in this crummy neighborhood. I'll take Ryan so you can finish putting in that insulation.

LARRY:
Later.

DORRIE:
You're supposed to be working, not reading. What is that, anyway?

LARRY:
A dictionary.

DORRIE:
Don't you know enough fancy words already?

LARRY:
I just want to understand what people are trying to say. . . . The other day Mrs. Wilson was ordering some flowers, and since it was so close to Christmas, I suggested poinsettias. She laughed at me. "Poinsettias at

this time of year! It's a little banal, don't you think?"
I didn't know what she meant, so I bought this pocket
dictionary. And I looked it up: "Banal: meaningless
from overuse, hackneyed, trivial." I've been learning
lots of words ever since. Words like . . .

DORRIE:
. . . upmarket. That's the word you ought to learn,
Larry. We've got to sell that pokey little place of ours
and move upmarket.

LARRY:
I've been working hard on it . . . it's starting to take
shape.

DORRIE:
You're talking about your goddamn maze, Larry, not
the house! Who's ever gonna buy a house that's got a
yard choked to the gill with bushes?

LARRY:
Shrubs.

DORRIE:
Well, we're not sleeping together any more, not until
you make up your mind to move . . .

LARRY:
. . . upmarket. *(LARRY joins MIDGE for coffee.)* She wants
to move upmarket, we've reached . . .

MIDGE:
. . . an impasse, fellow sibling, a dead-end . . . just like
your job.

LARRY:
I like my job.

MIDGE:
Larry, you're the branch manager of a so-so flower shop, and you've been there for fourteen years. You're going nowhere fast.

LARRY:
My life is shrinking before my eyes while my vocabulary is expanding. Isn't it weird?

MIDGE:
It's paradoxical. Just like it's paradoxical that I kicked my husband out because he was gay. I thought he didn't need me. And now I've moved in with him because he's gay, and he's sick, and he really does need me.

LARRY:
Paradoxical.

MIDGE:
Yeah. And highly ironic.

LARRY:
So how *is* Paul?

MIDGE:
He's dying, Larry . . . but they don't even have a name for it. You think if somebody was gonna die from something, it could at least have a name.

(LARRY returns to his maze.)

LARRY:

A paradoxical, banal upmarket impasse. That's my life on December 21, 1983 . . . the shortest day of the year . . . the winter solstice.

DORRIE *(opposite LARRY's singing)*:
I hadn't figured you for a show off when we met, Larry, so how come you're exploding these days with fancy words? Are you trying to put me down? You think you're smarter than me, don't you? Smarter than poor dumb Dorrie. You used to be fun, you know, you used to make me laugh, now all you talk about are turf mazes, knot gardens, shrubs, bushes, nothing but goddamn shrubs and bushes! I swear, Larry, one day I'm gonna get a bulldozer in there and clear the whole thing out.

LARRY *(opposite DORRIE's speech)*:
    Watching where I'm going,
    wondering where I've gone.
    Never really knowing
    but I keep moving on,
    I keep moving on,
    I keep moving on . . .

(As the speech and song rise to a climax, the sound that emerges is that of a bulldozer, drowning everything out with a tremendous crash. The ENSEMBLE destroy the maze.)

DORRIE:

I warned you, Larry. I told you it looked weird. It looked dumb. Besides, the neighbourhood's going downhill, the house is a dump anyway, and I'm just plain sick of it, you hear me? I'm sick of it, all of it.

(She turns away. LARRY kneels in the ruins of his maze.)

LARRY:
> Look at the sky.
> I thought I knew it so well.
> I never knew it was falling
> until it fell.
>
> Look at the time.
> I thought I'd share it with you.
> I never knew it was flying
> until it flew.
>
> Look at the sky,
> looking at me,
> walking away.
> Couldn't I try,
> couldn't I see,
> couldn't I stay?
>
> Wondering when,
> wondering how,
> and why.
> Look at us then,
> look at us now,
> look at the sky.
>
> Look at our love.
> I thought it went on and on.
> I never knew it was going
> till it was gone.
>
> Look at the sky,
> looking at me,
> walking away.

Couldn't I try,
couldn't I see,
couldn't I stay?

Wondering when,
wondering how,
and why.
Look at us then,
look at us now,
look at the sky.

DORRIE:
Look at our love.
I thought it went on and on.
I never knew it was going
till it was gone.

DORRIE AND LARRY:
Look at the sky,
looking at me,
walking away.
Couldn't I try,
couldn't I see,
couldn't I stay?

Wondering when,
wondering how,
and why.
Look at us then,
look at us now,
look at the sky,
look at the sky,
look at the sky . . .

(END OF SCENE)

Scene Six

LARRY'S FRIENDS

(HERSH is helping LARRY move.)

HERSH:
You loved her, pal. You *did* love her. That's something you're going to want to remember. It'll make all this seem worthwhile in the long run, the fact that you really did love her in the beginning.

LARRY:
I can't talk about it, Hersh.

HERSH:
You're gonna have to one day, Lorenzo, and the longer you wait, the harder it's gonna be.

LARRY:
I got a notebook. I thought I'd write down my feelings.

HERSH *(reading)*:
"Dorrie. Dorrie." That's it? That's all you've got to say?

LARRY:
For now.

HERSH:
Look, guy, we grew up next door to each other. We've been best friends for how long?

LARRY:
I don't know. Twenty years, maybe?

HERSH:
Twenty-three. If you can't tell me, then who can you tell?

LARRY:
No one, I guess.

HERSH:
Okay, pal. But don't forget us. Don't forget your friends . . .

(LARRY wanders to his parents' home for supper.)

STU:
And don't forget one thing, son. She knows how to manage money. She won't be bleeding you royal for the rest of your bloody life. Right, Mum?

DOT:
It's not my place to say, but I always thought she was such a tight wound-up little thing.

STU:
Now Mother . . .

DOT:
I'd rather be a dot than a door.

LARRY:
How are *you* feeling?

STU:
The same. A man works forty-five years without a day sick in his life, then he retires, and suddenly his gut aches like it's killing him . . .

LARRY:
You should see the Doctor.

STU:
Doctors. What do they know? It's Larry I'm worried about . . .

LARRY:
Don't worry about me.

(LARRY has joined MIDGE for a walk.)

MIDGE:
I'm not worried. Honestly, Lare-snare, you're well out of it. She's a total bitch. And on top of that she's brainless. And she tricked you into getting married. Why the hell wasn't she on the pill like every other woman in the universe? Because she's dumb, that's why. Dumb like a fox, that's what I think.

HERSH:
I was just thinking, Lorenzo, a three-year marriage that doesn't pan out isn't a tragedy.

LARRY:
It was five years, Hersh, five.

HERSH:
Oh. Sorry, pal.

(LARRY sits having tea with VIVIAN.)

VIVIAN:
Of course, no one ever understands other people's marriages, such terribly private arrangements, when you come to think of it. But still, you and Dorrie had different goals, and having different goals can be tough. I mean, let's face it: you married someone you had nothing in common with. Oh, to tell you the truth, I used to wonder what you saw in her . . . know what I mean?

(The stage is full of shadows, whispering to LARRY.)

ALL:
Be careful, Larry,

VIVIAN:
Be careful of silence.

MIDGE:
. . . of words.

HERSH:
. . . of other people.

DORRIE:
. . . of yourself.

LARRY:
    Lost my chance,
    lost my place,
    lost in time,
    lost in space . . .

(BRUCE and ERLEEN appear, 50ish, affable, lots of new money.)

BRUCE:
Larry Weller? Bruce Sztuwark. Play golf with Bill Herschel. Said we should get together. I'll cut to the chase. I got big money, a big house, a big garden. Said to Erleen, that's the wife, I didn't know what to do with any of it.

ERLEEN:
Not a clue, honey.

BRUCE:
Then we went to England . . .

ERLEEN:
We saw this maze . . .

BRUCE:
It blew us away!

ERLEEN:
Then I said to Bruce . . .

BRUCE:
. . . and I said to Erleen . . .

BOTH:
We oughta get ourselves one of these for home!

ERLEEN:
Can't you just imagine it?

BRUCE:
Hersh said you're the man.

LARRY:
But I've only made one maze . . . in my garden . . . and I didn't get to finish it.

ERLEEN:
But you *want* to make mazes, don't you?

LARRY:
Absolutely.

BRUCE:
Now you're talking!

ERLEEN (*easing LARRY to a drafting table*)**:**
You just sit down, honey, and design a maze like we've been dreaming about . . . like *you've* been dreaming about.

BRUCE:
'Cause you know what you are?

LARRY:
Very lucky?

BRUCE:
  You're the maker of mazes,

ERLEEN:
  you will lead us astray.

BRUCE:
Fill our lives with hidden turnings,

ERLEEN:
until we find the way.

LARRY (*shows them the design*):
How's that?

BRUCE:
Great!

(*The construction of the maze begins as the song continues.*)

BRUCE:
You're the maker of mazes,

ERLEEN:
you can help us get lost.

BRUCE:
Fill our lives with priceless yearnings,

ERLEEN:
but never count the cost.

LARRY:
Aren't you worried about . . . ?

(*BRUCE fills LARRY's hands with money, which he uses to pay the workers.*)

BRUCE AND ERLEEN:
>Architectural perfection,
>limitless direction.
>
>Build a dream with each design
>walk the path that's yours and mine.

MEN:
>'Cause you're the maker of mazes,

WOMEN:
>you will lead us astray.

MEN:
>Fill our lives with hidden turnings

ALL:
>undiscovered yearnings,
>we can turn and turn and turn
>until we find the way . . .

(The drafting table becomes a banquet table. The maze workers are now LARRY's friends and family.)

HERSH:
September 18, 1985.

LARRY:
I want to thank Bruce and Erleen for throwing this farewell party for me. Heck, I wouldn't be leaving if they hadn't got things started by hiring me to make my first maze . . .

BRUCE:
The first of many.

ERLEEN:
Here, here.

LARRY:
It's not Hampton Court yet, but I'm getting there.

DORRIE:
The best of luck. I'm sorry you're going.

LARRY:
I'll still see Ryan . . . all the weekends we can . . . and holidays, and summer.

DORRIE:
It's just Chicago, Larry, not the ends of the earth.

HERSH:
I guess it's an offer you can't refuse, Lorenzo.

LARRY:
It's a commission to build a maze for one of the richest men in America.

HERSH:
But you're leaving Winnipeg.

LARRY:
I'm thirty-five, Hersh.

HERSH:
So am I, buddy. You don't see me moving.

MIDGE:

Go for it. Get the hell out of here. I only wish I'd done it when I had the chance, and maybe I will yet. And look, I've got poor old Paul's money growing mold in the bank, you might as well take a chunk. He had a soft spot for you. You never stopped shaking hands with him like a lot of people did towards the end, scared shitless. You even hugged him once . . . that last week at the hospice. I was out in the corridor, but I saw it happen . . .

BRUCE:

Listen, everybody . . .

ERLEEN:

Be quiet all . . . Bruce has a speech.

BRUCE:

I want to say that this man sitting before you is a genius. You've seen the maze he's installed at our place . . . the colour photos in the paper and the spread in *Maclean's*. And now he's off to Chicago to build a maze for a guy with even more bucks than me! To think that this is the guy who created it all. Let's have a toast, ladies and gents. I give you Larry Weller, a great guy, and a masterly maker of mazes . . .

MEN:

'Cause you're the maker of mazes,

WOMEN:

you will lead us astray . . .

MEN:
> Fill your lives with hidden turnings

ALL:
> Undiscovered yearnings.
> we can turn and turn and turn,
> until we find the way . . .

(END OF SCENE)

Scene Seven

LARRY IN LOVE

ENSEMBLE:
Fifteen minutes
in the life,
in the life of Larry Weller.

MEN:
Ordinary fella,

WOMEN:
quiet kinda guy.

ENSEMBLE:
Funny how they send him
where the air is high . . .

DORRIE:
A cocktail party in suburban Chicago . . .

ENSEMBLE:
Larry Weller . .

CHARLOTTE:
An evening in summer, 1986.

ENSEMBLE:
Larry Weller . . .

(As cocktail music continues underneath, BETH steps from the crowd: bright, brittle, attractive, not yet 30.)

BETH:
So you're the man who leads people astray . . .

LARRY:
In a purely professional sense.

BETH:
I'm working on my doctoral thesis: *Women Saints and the Nature of Feminine Goodness.*

LARRY:
You're interested in puzzles . . . like me.

BETH:
I'm interested in anything I can't figure out immediately.

LARRY:
Maybe I should make a maze for you.

BETH:
What would my maze be like?

LARRY:
All mazes are the same . . . and different . . . fifteen turnings leading to a final destination, a goal . . .

BETH:
A prize?

LARRY:
Exactly. Something to reward the patience of those who have picked their way through the maze's path and arrived at the chosen place.

BETH:
You'll need patience to pick your way through to me. That's what my parents would say.

LARRY:
You still live at home?

BETH:
No. they finally pitched me out on my twenty-fifth birthday. That is, they sold their house and moved to a condo in Hawaii. I sort of, you might say, got the message.

LARRY:
I lived at home until I was twenty-six.

BETH:
Why?

LARRY:
I was happy, I guess. Or happy enough, anyway.

BETH:
How funny you should say that! That's what I'm going to call my thesis: *Happy Enough*.

LARRY:
Why?

BETH:
Because I believe that most of us have just enough happiness to keep us from toppling over into the abyss.

LARRY:
I'm not sure what abyss you're talking about . . .

BETH:
What finally made you leave home at twenty-six?

LARRY:
I got married.

BETH:
And your wife? Is she here with you?

LARRY:
We're divorced. She lives back in Winnipeg.

BETH:
Any children?

LARRY:
A son, Ryan . . . eight years old . . . he lives with his mother.

BETH:
You must find it terribly lonely.

LARRY:
I do. I am. I'm terribly lonely.

BETH:
You look as though you're about to say something.

LARRY:

Why don't we leave?

BETH:

Yes, why not? Let's get the hell out of here.

LARRY:

Not just yet . . . I have to claim my prize.

(They embrace and kiss as the ENSEMBLE change the cocktail party to the kitchen of their home. BETH is preparing her lunch.)

BETH:

> Sticks of carrot,
> cubes of cheese:
> little edible destinies.
>
> Slice of apple,
> bunch of grapes:
> pleasing patterns and soothing shapes.
>
> I put the world in order,
> neat and tight and trim.
> Praising God's creation,
> a secular Seraphim.
> So bless them all,
> each apple slice
> and every carrot stick.
> They keep away
> the gloom and doom.
> Hey, isn't that the trick?

I know the tough get going
when the going gets too tough.
But the ones like me,
duck every punch.
I bob and weave
and pack a lunch,
and I'm happy,
happy enough.

LARRY (*dressing for work*):
You look beautiful today.

BETH:
You know what Brigid felt about beauty?

LARRY:
Brigid who?

BETH:
St. Brigid . . . sixth-century Irish lass . . . very beautiful but extremely devout. She prayed to be made ugly so she could fend off her suitors.

LARRY:
Why?

BETH:
She wanted to marry God. . . . And her prayers were answered. One of her eyes grew enormously big and the other one disappeared, so her father said all right, you can be a nun.

LARRY:
A one-eyed nun.

BETH:
And then there was St. Lucy, third century. She was so sick of being told she was beautiful that she plucked out her eyes and threw them in her lover's face.

LARRY:
I guess that showed him.

BETH:
What these women wanted was spiritual purity. And the shortest route to heaven was a quickie divorce between the body and the spirit. Works for me.

> Holy women,
> lost in time;
> every one is a friend of mine.
> Mystic virgins,
> cryptic nuns:
> who'd have thought they're the lucky ones?
>
> I study all their struggles,
> chronicle each deed.
> Hoping for a hero
> who'll be just what I need.

(The women of the ENSEMBLE enter dressed as mediaeval saints, and function as a backup chorus for BETH.)

> So bless them all,
> each martyred saint

that history forgot.
They help me see
just what I am,
as well as what I'm not.

I know the tough get going
when the going gets too tough.
And those holy dames
were no one's fool.
They lost their lives
but kept their cool.
They were happy,
happy enough.

Not rapt,
transfigured or ecstatic.
That's too dramatic
for one like me.
I choose
the line of least resistance.
And my existence
is trouble-free.

LARRY *(ready to leave for work)*:
I don't mean to diminish your sanctity, but you're still beautiful.

BETH:
Was she beautiful?

LARRY:
Who?

BETH:
Dorrie.

LARRY:
She . . . she could be attractive.

BETH:
Fat or thin?

LARRY:
Skinny.

BETH:
A skinny car saleswoman. Wait, I'm getting an image. Lots of jangling jewelry, gobs of blue eye shadow. . . . Oh God, why am I jealous of her?

LARRY:
You shouldn't be. There's no reason. I love you. Very much. *(He kisses her and exits.)*

BETH:
So bless them all,
each apple slice
and every carrot stick.
They keep away
the gloom and doom.
Hey, isn't that the trick?

I know the tough get going
when the going gets too tough.
We're both out of step,
and kind of quaint.

You'll make your maze,
I'll seek my saint.
We'll be happy,
Yes, we'll be happy,
We'll be happy,
happy,
happy enough.

(END OF SCENE)

Scene Eight

LARRY, INC.

(STU is helped on by DOT. He's in great pain.)

MIDGE:
> Larry's pappy,
> such a happy chappy,
> loves his tiny tot.
>
> Hugs his missus,
> covers her with kisses,
> she's his darling Dot.
>
> Life's so cheery,
> never teary, dearie,
> sun is shining bright.
> but all of that can change in a single night.

DOT *(whispers to LARRY):*
He tires easily. Don't make him talk too much . . . but he'll be glad to see you.

STU:
What are you staring at? It's the bathrobe, isn't it? It's your mother's. She thought it'd be warmer for me . . . why waste money? I'm not going to be around much longer.

LARRY *(out of time, to us)*:

How could I answer that? I wasn't ready to grow up that much yet, to deal with the idea of my father dying. I wanted to ask him so much: how to be a son, how to be a father. But I didn't ask him anything. I told him things: that he looked great, that he'd be fine, and then I left . . .

(BETH joins LARRY as they travel.)

BETH:
Larry, I said I'd follow you to the ends of the earth . . . but to Memphis?

LARRY:
I go where the work is and this is where he lives.

BETH:
Where *who* lives?

LARRY:
His name's Johnny Q. Questly.

BETH:
Not for real . . .

LARRY:
Yes, for real. He's one of the biggest stars in Nashville, and he wants me to build a maze around the tomb of his wife, Queenie . . .

(JOHNNY Q. QUESTLY, 50ish, slightly over-the-hill country music star, enters carrying a guitar.)

JOHNNY *(overlapping)*:

. . . Queenie, she was one of God's own marching angels. Never took herself one look at another man in forty years of married life. Never a word of complaint when I was on the road, and I was on the road a hell of a lot. Forgiveness? She was a woman who knew the meaning of forgiveness, cause I messed up a coupla times, real bad . . . but she always knew I'd come home in the end. On our wedding anniversary one year, I bought her a necklace. Diamonds, all diamonds. Like the fella says, Diamonds are forever, but she only wore the damn thing once or twice and then she got the cancer and passed away. A simple life, that's what she liked, just the two of us out here, watching the sun go down. That's all I need, she used to tell me, just the two of us loving each other.

> Walkin' the walk
> though the way is windin'.
> Talkin' the talk
> with the best of friends.
> Makin' the most
> of the world I'm findin'.
> Ridin' the road,
> wond'rin' where it ends.
>
> Breakin' the rules
> quick as I can learn 'em.
> Borrowin' time
> that I can't repay.
> Crossin' each bridge
> just before I burn 'em.
> Lovin' my life
> every single day.

Ashes to ashes,
dust to dust,
that's the way the story goes.
Cradle to grave, we
spin the wheel,
where it stops, nobody knows.
Mornin' to mornin',
day to day,
growin' from year to year.
Ashes to ashes,
and dust to dust
just enjoy it while we're here.

LARRY (*showing him a sketch*)**:**
The maze I've planned is unicursal . . . a simple winding path without an alternate route. Like a coiled snake, or a seashell, or the birthing journey . . .

JOHNNY:
"The birthing journey." I like that. Queenie would've liked it, too.

Ashes to ashes,
and dust to dust
just enjoy it while we're here.

(*LARRY joins MIDGE, at STU's funeral.*)

MIDGE:
All I wanted was to have one conversation with the old bugger. We never did, you know, not once.

LARRY:
He wasn't much for words. I guess I take after him.

MIDGE:

It was different for you. He took you to all those football games when you were a kid.

LARRY:

That was a helluva long time ago.

MIDGE:

So did you do the father-son thing? Did you, like, really talk when you were sitting there in the stands, the two of you?

LARRY:

I don't think so. Maybe "Great play." Or "Lousy block." That was pretty much about it.

MIDGE:

It figures. . . . You know, even when Paul got AIDS, when he was in the hospice dying, our dear father Stu never once . . . he didn't even . . . he just . . . oh Christ, why did you get me started?

LARRY:

Midge, that's just the way he was.

MIDGE:

Do you think he and Mom ever had a conversation? I bet they didn't. I bet they just lived inside their dumb silence, all those years.

LARRY:

We can't know.

MIDGE:

What do you mean "we can't know"? What's that supposed to mean? Oh hell, what's any of it supposed to mean?

JOHNNY *(with LARRY echoing)*:
> Mornin' to mornin'
> day to day,
> growin' from year to year.

JOHNNY AND LARRY:
> Ashes to ashes,
> and dust to dust . . .

JOHNNY:
> just enjoy it while we're here.

LARRY:
> Ashes to ashes,
> and dust to dust . . .

(END OF SCENE)

Scene Nine

LARRY'S PENIS

STU:
August 17, 1990 . . . Larry's 40th birthday.

(People come and go rapidly, showering LARRY with gifts and good wishes.)

BETH:
Here, darling . . . it's Batty Langley's *New Principles of Gardening*, 1728 . . . the maze designs are extraordinary. I knew you'd love it.

HERSH:
Sorry I can't be there, Lorenzo . . . let's celebrate the next one together. Deal?

RYAN:
The tie is from me, Dad. I picked it out myself. Honest.

DORRIE:
The card is from me. That's what I do now. I'm the chief Canadian executive for SkyBlue Greetings. Hope you like it.

LARRY:
"Here's to being older and wiser. Affectionately, Dorrie."

MIDGE:

Hey, Lare, over the hump, eh? Life's great in Toronto. Have a new guy named Ian. You'll love him . . . he picked out this card: Forty. Four-T, get it? and the four T's are Taste, Talent, Technique and Testosterone . . . isn't that a scream?

DOT:

Here, son . . . it's a cheque for twenty dollars. Go have yourself a celebration. Take it from me, life really does begin at forty . . .

(LARRY and BETH are in their bedroom. They begin undressing and making love.)

ENSEMBLE:
> It's so fine
> to be here
> and in love
> and with you.
> It's all mine,
> it's all real,
> and it's all
> comin' true.
> Oh, oh, oh, oh, oh . . .

LARRY:

I'm sorry, Beth! Jesus I'm sorry . . . why does this keep happening lately?

BETH:

It's not your fault.

LARRY:

Well, it's not yours . . .

BETH:

Yes it is, actually. I blame myself for foisting that surprise party on you. Who wants to announce forty to the world? It's frightening. I can understand that.

LARRY:

Fine . . . but can you understand what it's like to feel lost all the time? To wake up in the middle of the night, stare out the window at the chipped moon and wonder just when my life began to drain away? I'm forty years old, and what do I do? I make mazes . . .

BETH:

Wonderful mazes! Like that one you just did for the children's hospital in Milwaukee? It's so beautiful! With a wishing well in the middle where they can toss their pennies and whisper their deepest desires. To get better. To live. To grow up. To be like everyone else.

LARRY:

You know what else I put in that maze, Beth? Four exits. Not one, not two, four. Do you know why I did that? So that no one could possibly get lost, really lost, like me.

BETH:

You're not lost! This is just a natural phase, a chapter, a passing condition . . .

LARRY:

Stop it, Beth. Just stop it.

BETH:

Listen to me, Larry, there was a sixth-century martyr named St. Guignolé, and there's a wooden statue of him in a church in France.

LARRY:

So?

BETH:

Well, this wooden statue has an upright wooden member, and thousands of visitors of both sexes have made pilgrimages to it over the years in order to whittle away at good old St. Guignolé's upright dingle. They carry home the sawdusty bits, boil it up in a broth and drink it for supper.

LARRY:

Are you suggesting that we make an emergency pilgrimage to . . . ?

BETH:

No, Larry, I'm not. The point is that this, this thing, this whatever it is that's worrying you is an ancient and universal concern. Potency. Fertility. It's just the old fear-of-death image in disguise.

LARRY:

Ah, so that's what it is!

BETH:

You're an absolutely normal and typical human being . . .

LARRY:
Thanks.

BETH:
I'll finish getting undressed, and we'll try again.
Everything will be fine, you'll see, just say a prayer to
St. Guignolé . . .

MEN'S VOICES:
Welcome to Larry's Penis.

LARRY:
It isn't quite awake.

(The WOMEN's voices provide a mocking choral counterpoint.)

MEN'S VOICES:
His lightning rod,
his family jewels,
his one-eyed trouser snake.

LARRY:
It isn't quite awake.

MEN'S VOICES:
His ding-dong-bell,
his billy-boy,
his turkey neck surprise.

LARRY:
Welcome to Larry's Penis.

LARRY AND MEN'S VOICES:
There's no need to rise . . .

(SALLY appears from the past: a ripe straightforward Winnipeg girl in her early 20's.)

SALLY:
The minute you walked in the room, I said to myself, "Sally Wolsche, that is the cutest boy in the whole Floral Arts Class." Of course, there's only one other boy *in* the class, and he's as queer as a kipper.

LARRY:
Really? How do you know?

SALLY:
I can tell from the way he moves his ass. I can tell a lot about a guy from that, and I sure like the way you move yours. Hey, what's with the blushing? You haven't had much experience, have you, honey? Don't worry, Sally will teach you what she knows, and she knows plenty . . .

You and I
in the backseat of a car.
Although we're goin' nowhere,
we're goin' pretty far.
You and I
at the point of no return,
with a whole new lot of lessons
we can learn.

Let me hold you in my arms
for just a minute,
Let me memorize the look
in your eyes.
Put your hand in mine, and then

we can begin it.
Later on, we'll think about goodbyes.
Let me know you
show you,
make the world seem right.
Let me teach you,
reach you,
Let me hold you in my arms
tonight.

(DORRIE enters from the past, ready for bed.)

DORRIE:
You and I
in a squeaky double bed.
Although we're just beginning,
we've got our lives ahead.
You and I
fit together like a dream.
Are these marriage vows as easy
as they seem?

Let me hold you in my arms
for just an hour.
Let me lie here by your side
for a while.
Just pretend that you and I
are like a flower,
you were meant to rearrange in style.
Let me take you,
make you
cling to me so tight.
Let me see you,

free you.
Let me hold you in my arms
tonight.

SALLY AND DORRIE:
What a revelation,
how it's burning bright!
What a sweet sensation
in the lonely autumn night.
A piece of pure perfection,
a part of heaven's plan.
It's there in the connection
of a woman and a man . . .

(BETH re-enters, having changed to a negligée.)

BETH:
You and I
on an eiderdown duvet.
Although we've got forever,
we take it day by day.
You and I
seem as though we have it planned.
but there's so much we can never
understand.

Let me hold you in my arms
until the morning.
Let me listen to the sound
of your sleep.
For the dawn can fill the sky
without a warning,
and the dreams you dream alone won't keep.

Let me feel you,
heal you,
turn the dark to light.
Let me lead you,
need you.
Let me hold you in my arms
tonight.

SALLY, DORRIE AND BETH:
What a revelation,
how it's burning bright!
What a sweet sensation
in the lonely autumn night.
A piece of pure perfection,
a part of heaven's plan.
It's there in the connection
of a woman and a man . . .

ALL THREE:
Let me see you,
free you,
make the world seem right.
Let me know you,
show you..
Let me hold you in my arms
tonight.

(END OF SCENE)

Scene Ten

LARRY SO FAR

DORRIE:
O'Hare Airport, Chicago . . . August, 1993 . . . Ryan's annual summer visit. He's fifteen.

(DORRIE and LARRY are on the phone.)

LARRY:
I think I should finally tell him about us.

DORRIE:
What about us?

LARRY:
About our getting married. About his birth.

DORRIE:
Oh.

LARRY:
I just wanted to know what you think.

DORRIE:
I think you shouldn't.

LARRY:
But why not?

DORRIE:
What good could that possibly do him?

(RYAN appears. He's now fifteen.)

RYAN:
> Nickels and dimes
> ring in my pocket,
> pieces of time
> ring in my head . . .

(LARRY is waiting at the airport.)

LARRY:
When Ryan was five he told me . . .

RYAN:
I've got voices in my head, and they're talking all the time.

LARRY:
At first I was scared, and then I knew what he meant. He was thinking . . . just like me. People think I'm being quiet. But it isn't quiet. Not inside my head . . . It's like every time I go to meet Ryan at the airport. The same thing happens. I'm afraid of being late, so I get there way too early. I buy a magazine, but I never open it. I order a drink, but I never touch it. I just sit, and wait . . .

> Listening to the musak,
> looking at the signs,
> telling me that Flight Three-Oh-Three

86

from the Peg's gonna be a bit late.
Planning my performance,
thinking of my lines:
leaping through that hoop full of fears when
my son first appears at the gate.

Staring at the crowd,
wondering if he'll see me.
Tentative but proud,
hoping that he'll be me,
hoping that will free me . . .

Larry so far,
so much I'll never know.
Larry so far,
and farther still to go.

Yes, I've been waiting for you,
about a million years.
Then all at once a mirror
amazingly appears.

'Cause now you're here,
you're in my sight, you're in my
mind and heart.

Don't know where I am going,
Don't know what I should do.
You're flying while I'm falling,
and calling out to you.

Maybe you and I can really try
to make a brand new start.

Larry so close
Larry so near,
Larry so far . . .

RYAN:
Every time I visit, I have to remind myself what he looks like.

DORRIE:
But you see him every year.

RYAN:
He changes. So do I. Anyway, what I *really* remember is when I was little. Before he left. When he'd wheel me around in my stroller through that crazy maze of his.

DORRIE:
I remember it too.

RYAN:
Is that why you never finished tearing it down? Why you kept it all these years.

DORRIE:
You'll miss your plane.

RYAN:
I never do.

LARRY:
The woman that you marry
is part of you for life.

The mother of your children,
the memory of your wife.

I'll take the hope you carry,
and all the love you bring.
We'll ride the roller coaster,
we'll grab the golden ring

For you'll show me why I know that I
belong right where you are.

Larry so close, Larry so near.
Larry so close, Larry so near . . .

RYAN:
Hi, Dad.

LARRY:
Larry so far.

(LARRY, RYAN stand looking at each other, waiting, not know-ing what to say or do.)

(End of ACT I)

ACT II

Scene One

LARRY'S KID

(The music underneath indicates that action continues where it stopped at the end of Act I.)

LARRY:
Hi there, fella.

RYAN:
Hey, Dad.

LARRY:
So how's your Mom?

RYAN:
Okay.

LARRY:
We're going to have the best time, son. Absolutely. We'll go the Aquarium, and a ball game, and . . .

RYAN:
Dad, we do the same stuff every summer. Kid stuff.

LARRY:
Well, what would you like to do?

RYAN:
I want to see you work. I want to watch you build one of your mazes.

LARRY:
You really do?

RYAN:
I really do.

LARRY:
Okay. Great. And then maybe we can have a talk.

RYAN:
About what?

(DORRIE is on the phone again with LARRY.)

DORRIE:
He knows about sex, Larry, if that's what you're talking about. He's known for years. I bought him a book.

LARRY:
That's not what I mean.

DORRIE:
No. No. I don't want you to tell him about that. He probably knows already.

LARRY:
How could he?

DORRIE:
There've been hints. Questions.

LARRY:
What kind of questions?

DORRIE:
Like why we got divorced.

LARRY:
What did you say to that one?

DORRIE:
I said I was too dumb to be married at that time in my life.

LARRY:
So was I. Christ. A regular doofus . . .

DORRIE:
No, Larry. We were both dumb, but I was also stupid and also . . .

LARRY:
You're too hard on yourself.

DORRIE:
. . . and also crazy. But then I got sane. I figured it out, Larry, after you left, all those years. I figured out how to stop being a coupon-cutter and get sane and stay that way. And one of the things I figured out was that you don't have to know every single particle of

everything. Not every last shred has to be dragged out in the open. And I don't want Ryan to think . . . to think we had to, you know, get married, that we were forced to . . .

LARRY:
We loved each other, Dorrie. That's the real reason we got married.

DORRIE:
Did we?

LARRY:
Yes we did. I may have forgotten a lot, but I remember that for sure.

DORRIE:
Just this one thing, Larry. Trust me on this one.

LARRY:
If you're sure.

DORRIE:
I'm sure.

LARRY:
Okay.

(*DORRIE hangs up the phone.*)

DORRIE:
Where did it start?
Where was the rest of my life

after he walked out the door?
What did I do?
Gave him the best of my life,
couldn't provide any more.

I still can remember
each one of those empty mornings
here all alone
with my hand on the phone.

What I believe
is you just do what you can.
'Cause you're living your life
without the dream of a man.
No more caring,
sharing,
wearing your heart on your sleeve.
Girl, here's looking at you,
yeah, you're gonna come through.
It's what I believe.

Who am I now
now that I'm out on my own?
Trying to ride from the past.
Why am I here,
facing each doubt on my own?
Learning to fly much too fast.

I still can remember
each one of those endless evenings
here in my bed,
with the dawn still ahead.

What I believe
is you just live day by day.
With a child you will raise
and a home where you'll stay.
No denying,
crying,
trying a reason to grieve.
Girl, here's looking at you,
yeah you're gonna come through.
It's what I believe.

After we stopped pretending,
gave up the happy ending,
lost all the love we had so long ago.
Tell me what's left in store now.
Isn't there something more now?
Let me know,
then let me go.

It's what I believe.

No more caring,
sharing,
wearing your heart on your sleeve.
Girl, here's looking at you,
yeah, you're gonna come through.
I am looking at me.
And I like what I see
It's what I believe
it's what I believe.

(END OF SCENE)

Scene Two

LARRY'S TRAVELS

(We're in BETH and LARRY's kitchen, overflowing with papers, forms, etc.)

BETH:
What's happening to me? Miss Every-Apple-Slice and Carrot-Stick-in-Its-Place has just rewritten her Guggenheim application for the forty-first time.

LARRY:
Then let me take it and mail it before you rewrite it for the forty-second time.

BETH:
Don't touch that! Look at me. This Guggenheim has driven me gaga. . . . Or should that be gugu? . . . You never get my jokes.

LARRY:
Beth, I'm worried about you . . .

BETH:
There's nothing to be worried about.

LARRY:
You're counting on this fellowship so much. What if you don't get it?

BETH:

Don't be ridiculous. Of course I'm going to get it. I'm widely read, committed, and clear-eyed, I can't miss!

LARRY:

Maybe we should have another plan.

BETH:

Don't be silly. What other plan could we possibly have?

LARRY:

Well, maybe if I applied for a grant myself . . .

BETH:

Don't be ridiculous, Larry. . . . Now, I think we should list the house with a good rental agency right away. You have to start early with these things, you have to plan ahead . . .

(The ENSEMBLE become a group of cultural bureaucrats.)

WOMEN:

Dear Dr. Prior . . .

SOLO WOMAN:

Unfortunately, an unprecedented number of applications were received this year . . .

MEN:

Dear Mr. Weller . . .

SOLO MAN:

Our heartiest congratulations on your successful application.

BETH:
You didn't tell me you applied.

LARRY:
I tried to.

BETH:
Jesus . . .

LARRY:
I didn't think I had much of a chance.

BETH:
It isn't as though you've actually published anything.

LARRY:
And I certainly don't have a PhD.

BETH:
Damn, damn, damn, damn.

LARRY:
Look, Beth . . .

BETH:
It isn't fair. Even you can see it isn't fair.

LARRY:
No, it isn't fair, you're right. But we can share it. That's what I'd always planned.

BETH:
That's ridiculous! I find it . . . humiliating.

LARRY:
Why humiliating?

BETH:
That you would have done this behind my back.

LARRY:
I didn't think of it that way.

BETH:
A breach of trust. That's what it really amounts to.

LARRY:
I'm sorry, Beth. You know I'd never . . .

BETH:
No, I don't know that. And I'm not sure you're sorry.

LARRY:
I just thought . . .

BETH:
What did you think? I'd be interested in knowing.

LARRY:
You seemed to want to go so terribly much.

BETH:
It wasn't just the going, Larry. God! It was — I don't know — the having.

LARRY:
But in a way we're both having.

BETH:
You just don't get it, do you?

LARRY:
Maybe I don't. Maybe there's a lot that I don't "get." That I never "got."

BETH:
Damn, damn, damn.

LARRY:
I'll show you England. I'll take you to Hampton Court. You can see where it all started for me. Why don't we just back our bags and go tomorrow?

BETH:
Tomorrow's not possible. How could we possibly . . . ?

LARRY:
Next week, then.

BETH:
I don't know.

LARRY:
Beth . . .

BETH:
Well, it's a good thing I listed the house. You wanted me to wait, remember? I told you we should go ahead.

LARRY:
We'll have a terrific time!

(The ENSEMBLE take us to Hampton Court once again.)

    We will go round and round again,
    follow along and come with me . . .

ENSEMBLE:
    . . . as we go round and round
    and round and round and round again . . .

LARRY:
A maze is designed so that we get to be part of the art.

BETH:
So you think this is an art, do you?

LARRY:
The whole thing about mazes is that they make perfect sense only when you look down on them from above.

BETH:
Like God in His heaven, you mean. Being privy to the one authentic map of the world.

LARRY:
Something like that.

BETH:
So what kind of a God wants us to get confused and keep us in a state of confusion?

LARRY:
Isn't that what we've always had? Chaos from the first day of creation? But mazes are an escape from

confusion. An orderly path for the persevering. Procession without congestion.

BETH:
You read that somewhere.

LARRY:
Probably.

BETH:
Well, at least they provide a way out.

LARRY:
One exit anyway.

BETH:
And what is it, my dearest Larry? Salvation or death? Or more confusion?

(STU, DOT, MIDGE, DORRIE and RYAN appear to LARRY.)

FAMILY:
. . . as we go round and round
and round and round and round again . . .

HERSH:
March 14, 1996.

HARRIET *(British academic, 50ish)*:
Dr. Prior, it's Harriet Ravenscourt, from the University of Sussex.

BETH:

Larry, they want me to be head of their Women's Studies department, just like that!

LARRY:

Let's not rush into anything, Beth.

HARRIET:

The salary's not bad.

BETH:

God, it's amazing!

HARRIET:

Secretarial staff of three.

BETH:

Three!

HARRIET:

And five teaching staff . . .

BETH:

. . . plus four cross-appointments!

HARRIET:

So you'll accept?

BETH:

This kind of thing doesn't come along all that often!

LARRY:

And what about us?

BETH:

Oh, Larry . . . there really hasn't been an "us" for a while now, has there?

LARRY:

I guess not.

HERSH:

Larry flew back to Chicago.

HARRIET:

There was a fax waiting for him.

BETH:

Just sell the furniture. Or keep what you want.

HERSH:

And then, a little later on . . .

HARRIET:

She sent him a letter.

BETH:

Darling Larry . . . all this will be easier for you if you think of life as a book each of us must write alone, and how, within that book, there are many chapters . . .

HARRIET:

He couldn't finish reading it . . .

HERSH:

. . . at least, not then.

LARRY:

Once again I'm off and running,
and I don't know where I'm heading,
but that only means I'm going twice as fast.

I don't even have the question,
but I'm looking for an answer
to the future in the present and the past.

I can stand here in the silence
till I feel my heart is beating,
But I've never known just what it's beating for.

Now I'm seven miles high
all alone here in the sky
and I'll never say goodbye
any more.

Close the book,
Shut the door
Pack your bag
Cut the string,
Everything.

Grab the key,
Turn your back
Walk away,
Walk away,
Walk away,
Walk away.

If I find the words are worthless,
if the feelings all seem empty,

then I'll concentrate on what I am instead.

I'll continue on this journey
to the centre of my being
through the never-ending pounding in my head.

There's a truth beyond illusion,
there's a rage beyond emotion,
there's a passion that keeps breaking down the door.

And I never found out why
I'm still seven miles high.
but you'll never see me cry
any more.

Crack the code,
break the spell,
make the move,
kill the pain,
start again.

Take your heart,
keep your pride,
Walk away,
Walk away,
Walk away,
Walk away.

Take the past and send it flying,
call this living worst than dying.
I'm not seven miles high
anymore ...

(END OF SCENE)

Scene Three

LARRY'S LONGINGS

(The ENSEMBLE help move LARRY through time and space once more.)

ENSEMBLE:
Fifteen minutes
in the life,
in the life of Larry Weller.

DORRIE:
A restaurant in downtown Toronto.

ENSEMBLE:
Larry Weller . . .

RYAN:
April, 1997.

ENSEMBLE:
Larry Weller . . .

(IAN — about 50, too eager to please — leads LARRY into a crowded bar.)

IAN:

Larry Weller, right? I'm Ian Stoker, Midge's friend. She asked me to keep an eye out for you while she parks the car.

LARRY:

Good to meet you, Ian . . . boy, this place is packed!

IAN:

That's Toronto for you. Everybody has to discover the same bar on the same weekend, or they don't feel connected.

LARRY:

I feel connected.

MIDGE:

Baby, brother! Let me look at you. Not bad for a double divorcée. Still looking?

LARRY:

I don't think so.

MIDGE:

You're still breathing? You're still looking. That's what this evening's for . . . we've got somebody for you to meet. Charlotte Angus. A terrific woman, am I right, Ian?

IAN:

Just terrific.

MIDGE:
I'm glad you moved here. I worried about you after Beth moved out . . .

LARRY:
I'm just fine.

MIDGE:
No you're not, Lare . . .

LARRY:
Okay . . . I could use a little warmth right about now.

MIDGE:
I knew it! Don't worry, Ian and I will give you lots, and Charlotte will provide the rest. There she is! *(We spot CHARLOTTE. Late 40's, attractive, carefully put together.)* A wonderful laugh, good taste in scarves, and hair colouring. You'll love her.

LARRY:
I don't think I have a choice.

MIDGE:
Larry, this is Charlotte.

IAN:
Charlotte, this is Larry.

MIDGE:
You look great, Charlotte.

IAN:
Like always.

MIDGE:
How's the job?

IAN:
Charlotte's in counselling.

MIDGE:
And say, bro, have you hung up your shingle yet?

IAN:
Larry's in mazes.

MIDGE:
Do you like Toronto?

IAN:
How does it compare to Chicago?

MIDGE:
Much theatre in Chicago?

IAN:
Great theatre here.

MIDGE:
Have you seen *Ragtime*, Larry?

IAN:
Have you seen it, Charlotte?

MIDGE:
No? Well don't worry . . .

IAN:
we've got two tickets right here.

BOTH:
Enjoy the show.

MIDGE:
I think they're getting along very well.

(LARRY and CHARLOTTE, left alone, walk together.)

CHARLOTTE:
They were right. It was an excellent show. Thank you for taking me.

LARRY:
I'm glad you liked it. But maybe we should thank Midge.

CHARLOTTE:
Her heart is in the right place.

LARRY:
Midge's heart has always been in the right place. It's her head that worries me. She is right, though. You have a wonderful laugh.

CHARLOTTE:
Thank you.

LARRY:
Would you like a nightcap?

CHARLOTTE:
I'd love one. So. *(They sit down at a table.)* Tell me about Larry.

LARRY:
He's forty-seven years old, he's been divorced twice
. . . and most of the time he thinks he doesn't want to
trust another person . . . ever again. Now tell me about
Charlotte.

CHARLOTTE:
What's there to tell?

> I wear a scarf,
> I dress in pink.
> I watch my weight,
> I take my zinc.
> I pop a pill
> I sip a drink,
> and I do fine.
>
> I hit the spa
> I keep in tone.
> I write a note,
> I use the phone.
> I love my friends,
> I live alone,
> and I do fine.
>
> Yes, I try
> to ease the life I live
> In a million different ways.
> All the little lost nights,
> all the little lost dawns
> all the little lost days.

I have a job,
I pay my way.
I read a book,
I catch a play.
I carve a path.
I walk each day,
and I do fine.

I own a house,
I keep it bright.
I greet each day,
I meet each night.
I shut the door
I dim the light,
and I do fine.

Yes, I try
to fill the emptiness
and to guard against the tears.
All the little lost days,
all the little lost weeks,
all the little lost years.

Some days
are harder than others
some nights
they never do end.
Some years
you think you'll break
before you bend.

You share a life
for twenty years.
You keep the hopes,

you hide the fears,
but then one day,
it disappears.
And I do fine.

My husband died
four years ago.
The cancer came
and didn't go.
Yes there's a lot
I never show,
and I do fine.

But I think
about the universe
full of husbands
and their wives.
All the little lost days,
all the little lost years . . .

Some days
are harder than others
some nights
they never do end.
Some years
you think you'll break
before they're gone.
But I go on,
yes, I go on.

I have a job,
I pay my way.
I read a book,
I catch a play.

I carve a path
I walk each day.

For although
this life's a battlefield,
I believe that love survives
all the little lost days
all the little lost years,
all the little lost lives.

(END OF SCENE)

Scene Four

LARRY'S LIVING TISSUES

(LARRY and CHARLOTTE are still sitting at the table.)

WAITER:
August 26, 1998.

LARRY:
Ham and cheese on rye.

CHARLOTTE:
Larry . . .

LARRY:
Turkey breast on rye . . . hold the mayo.

CHARLOTTE:
I'll have a small Caesar. It's too hot for anything else.

WAITER:
Anything to drink?

LARRY AND CHARLOTTE:
Perrier.

WAITER:
Coming right up.

CHARLOTTE:
Listen to the two of us . . . just over a year, and already we sound like an old married couple.

LARRY:
No we don't. This is . . . this is sweeter than a marriage.

CHARLOTTE:
Darling, what do you mean?

LARRY:
No lies, no theatrics, no staged manipulations . . .

CHARLOTTE:
Is that what your marriages were like? I'm sorry for you . . .

LARRY:
What about Derek?

CHARLOTTE:
He was the kindest of men. He never caused me a moment's pain in twenty years.

LARRY:
Do you still miss him?

CHARLOTTE:
Less and less each day.

LARRY:
Will you be coming over tonight?

CHARLOTTE:
If you like . . .

LARRY:
I like a lot.

CHARLOTTE:
What's on for you this afternoon?

LARRY:
Garth McCord is coming by.

CHARLOTTE:
Is everything nearly settled?

LARRY:
Not yet. He's very rich and very powerful, and very used to having his own way about every single detail. He loves flagstone, but he hates forsythia . . .

(McCORD barges in, almost 60, brusque, abrasive, used to being in charge.)

McCORD *(overlapping)*:
. . . forsythia. It's such a goddamn suburban shrub. This has got to be a classy maze, Weller. Classy, low-key, elegant . . .

LARRY:
We're in total agreement, Mr. McCord.

McCORD:
I told you to call me Garth.

LARRY:

I can't call you Garth if you keep calling me Weller.

McCORD:

What's your goddamn first name anyway? I forgot it.

LARRY:

Larry.

McCORD:

Look, Larry, remember how you described it to me? It was beautiful. What did you call it? "An extension of . . . "

LARRY AND McCORD:

" . . . a dreamy organic world."

McCORD:

Perfection. Brilliant. You're a genius. But no forsythia.

LARRY:

You have to let me build it the way I see it, Mr. McCord. Oh, I know, it's your cash, but it's my imagination. You're the maker of money . . .

And I'm the maker of mazes,
I will lead you astray.
Fill your life with hidden turnings,
until you find the way.

I'm the maker of mazes,
I can help you get lost.
Fill your life with priceless yearnings,
but never count the cost.

Architectural perfection,
limitless direction, limitless direction.

(LARRY starts to grow unsteady. He clutches his desk for support.)

McCord:
Larry?

Larry:
Limitless . . .

McCord:
Larry?

Larry:
Limitless . . .

McCord:
Are you okay?

Larry *(almost incoherent)*:
You can turn and turn and turn
You can turn and turn and turn
You can turn and turn and turn
and turn and turn and turn and . . .

(LARRY collapses. His desk becomes a hospital bed. A DOCTOR in her 30's is checking his reports.)

Doctor:
His vital signs are all strong . . .

Midge:
But he's still in a coma.

CHARLOTTE:
What caused it?

DOCTOR:
It could be a form of encephalitis . . . usually from a mosquito bite.

IAN:
Our fishing trip at Rice Lake.

CHARLOTTE:
Is he going to get better?

DOCTOR:
I can't say. I just can't say.

MIDGE:
I'm sorry, honey.

DOCTOR:
Have you contacted all other relatives?

CHARLOTTE:
Both his ex-wives were notified. They sent the flowers.

DOCTOR:
What about the rest of the family?

MIDGE:
Only Mum's left . . . and she's so sick, I don't want to tell her.

DOCTOR:
Anyone else?

RYAN: *(entering quietly)*
His son.

MIDGE:
Ryan! Charlotte, this is Ryan . . .

CHARLOTTE:
Your father loves you very much.

RYAN:
That's why I came here. That's why I'm staying here.

MIDGE:
But what about school?

RYAN:
I'm not leaving this room until he wakes up.

DOCTOR:
That may take a very long time.

RYAN:
I'm not going anywhere. This is where I belong.
Don't worry, Dad, you'll be fine.

> I'm a part of you now,
> you're a part of me.
> pieces of a puzzle
> no one else can see.

Petals of a flower,
ripples on a stream.
Shadows in the twilight,
voices in a dream.

Who could understand it?
Who would want to try?
Let me hold the moment
as it hurries by.

Pieces of a puzzle
no one else can see.
I'm a part of you now
you're a part of me.

(A vision of STU appears and joins RYAN.)

STU AND RYAN:
There's a thread
that ties a father to his son,
strong as steel,
thin as air.

And I know
that now your life has just begun
in my arms
in my care.

(STU vanishes.)

MIDGE:
Ryan, honey . . . it's been three weeks now.

RYAN:
Twenty-two days.

DOCTOR:
And there's no change in his condition.

RYAN:
He can hear me. I know he can.

> Pieces of a puzzle
> no one else can see.
> I'm a part of you now,
> you're a part of me.

LARRY *(slowly waking up)*:
Ryan? Midge? Charlotte? Ian? Where am I? Where have I been?

DOCTOR:
You've been in a coma, Mr. Weller. For twenty-two days.

RYAN:
What was it like, Dad?

LARRY:
Dark. Soft. Silent. Safe.

RYAN:
Like a maze, Dad.

(The ENSEMBLE take us from the hospital to the next location.)

ENSEMBLE *(in counterpoint)*:
> You can turn and turn and turn,
> you can turn and turn and turn,
> you can turn and turn and turn,
> until you find the way . . .

(END OF SCENE)

Scene Five

LARRY'S LOSS

(We're in a hospital corridor.)

DOT:
October 29, 1999.

DORRIE:
Poor Dot.

DOCTOR:
She was a grand old lady.

MIDGE:
She was ready to go.

DORRIE:
The last few months were so sad. . . . I'd sit with her, hold her hand, just be there.

MIDGE:
The two of you used to hate each other.

DORRIE:
People change, Midge.

MIDGE:
Lord, don't they . . .

DOCTOR:
I suppose she would want cremation, like Mr. Weller?

MIDGE:
Absolutely.

DORRIE:
Isn't it funny how she and Stu were so traditional about everything else, except this.

LARRY:
Not really. You never heard her talk when we were kids.

DOT (*as a vision*):
We're all dust in the end, children. Remember that, nothing but dust.

(*LARRY and MIDGE stand on a desolate lakeshore.*)

LARRY:
Two hours drive to West Hawk Lake. It always seems to take longer.

MIDGE:
God, it's windy out here! And grey, grey, grey . . .

LARRY:
It always looks like that just before the first snow. Remember when we put Dad's ashes here?

MIDGE:
Oh Jesus, Larry . . . hey, where's the urn?

LARRY:
I thought you put it in.

MIDGE:
I thought you did.

LARRY:
She must still be there on Dorrie's porch . . .

MIDGE:
I can't bear this.

LARRY:
We don't have to put her in the lake. It was only **an** idea . . .

MIDGE:
It looks too cold anyway.

LARRY:
Those waves . . .

MIDGE:
Larry? What if we . . .

LARRY:
. . . took her back to Toronto? I don't know.

MIDGE:
We could put her in my backyard. That nice place by the peonies.

LARRY:
She loved peonies.

MIDGE:

Or is it too ghoulish for words? Putting your mother's remains in your yard . . .

LARRY:

I don't think so. I mean, we may not want to admit it, but she's only . . .

MIDGE:

Ashes.

LARRY:

That's right. Dust.

(LARRY switches on the car radio.)

MIDGE:

No. We can't do it. We'd never feel right about it. We can't take her to Toronto. She hated Toronto. We'll have to get her ashes, come back and put 'em here in the lake.

RADIO ANNOUNCER:

CKLQ in Kenora, Hot for Country, 880 on your AM dial . . . it's minus 5 out there, and time to warm things up with Johnny Q. Questly and "Ashes To Ashes."

LARRY:

He sang this for me, Midge.

MIDGE:

What?

LARRY:
I made a maze for him . . . in Nashville . . . almost ten years ago . . . and he sang me this song . . .

MIDGE:
I hate country music.

LARRY:
Listen to the words, Midge . . .

SINGERS:
Walkin' the walk

JOHNNY:
though the way is windin'.

SINGERS:
Talkin' the talk

JOHNNY:
with the best of friends.

SINGERS:
Makin' the most

JOHNNY:
of the world I'm findin'.
Ridin' the road,
wond'rin' where it ends.

JOHNNY AND SINGERS:
Ashes to ashes,
and dust to dust,
that's the way the story goes.

JOHNNY:
>Cradle to grave, we
>spin the wheel . . .

LARRY AND JOHNNY:
>where it stops, nobody knows.

ALL *(except MIDGE)*:
>Mornin' to mornin',
>and day to day . . .

JOHNNY:
>Growin' from year to year . . .

MIDGE:
>Growing from year to year!

ALL:
>Ashes to ashes,
>and dust to dust,
>just enjoy it while we're here,
>just enjoy it while we're here,
>just enjoy it while we're here.

(END OF SCENE)

Scene Six

LARRY'S PARTY

(We're in LARRY's Toronto apartment, back where the play began.)

CHARLOTTE:
>Welcome to Larry's Party,
>the evening has begun.
>The guests have met,
>the table's set,
>and there's room for everyone . . .

BETH:
Dearest Larry . . .

DORRIE:
I'll be in Toronto next weekend . . .

BETH:
. . . for a visit . . .

DORRIE:
. . . on business . . .

BETH:
. . . so why don't the two of us . . .

DORRIE:
. . . get together for old time's sake?

BOTH:
Let me know.

CHARLOTTE:
How wonderful!

LARRY:
It's just a coincidence.

CHARLOTTE:
It's the perfect excuse to give a party.

LARRY:
You really think that's a good reason? To welcome both my ex-wives?

CHARLOTTE:
All right, then, to celebrate the opening of the McCord maze.

GARTH:
That's a goddamn great idea. We can lift a glass to celebrate and you can finally meet Marcia, my better half.

MARCIA:
I've actually met Larry before, Garth, at that cute little reception you threw at Prego, remember? The one with . . .

GARTH:
We'd love to come, Larry. Count us in.

CHARLOTTE:
Who else?

LARRY:
I'd like to have Midge and Ian there . . . just for security.

MIDGE:
Dorrie and Beth in the same room for the first time? Wild horses couldn't keep me away . . .

IAN:
I hope you behave, Midge.

MIDGE:
I *always* behave, Ian. That's my problem.

IAN:
One of them.

CHARLOTTE:
And what about that charming horticulturist from Spain who's helping you finish off the maze?

LARRY:
Sam? Sam Alvero? Why not? Give him a chance to sample the North American social whirl at its best.

CHARLOTTE:
This isn't the time for male jocularity.

LARRY:
When is?

CHARLOTTE:
Never. I thought you knew. There's a new by-law.

LARRY:
The table looks beautiful. Thanks for bringing the flowers.

CHARLOTTE:
I remembered what you said once about not having roses on a dinner table . . . the smell getting into the soup.

LARRY:
My days as a florist! We must have learned that in the first term. It's with you forever. . . . It's all with you forever, isn't it? Every bit of it . . .

CHARLOTTE:
There. Now we're ready.

LARRY:
April 26, the year 2000.

CHARLOTTE:
The tone is light,
the mood is right,
the night is bright and clear.
Welcome to Larry's Party,
I'm so glad you're here . . .

BETH:
Larry!

LARRY:
You're the first to arrive.

BETH:
I hoped we could talk.

LARRY:
Actually, Charlotte is here.

BETH:
Charlotte?

LARRY:
A friend.

BETH:
The plot thickens.

LARRY:
And Dorrie is coming too.

BETH:
Dorrie. Oh.

LARRY:
I hope this isn't going to be awkward.

BETH:
Not at all, Larry. Heavens, no.

SAM:

My dear friend, this is most generous of you.

LARRY:

Samuel Alvero, this is Beth Prior. Sam's been working with me on my latest maze. He's from Spain. Seville, isn't it, Sam? Beth has just come from London.

SAM:

I am enchanted to meet you.

BETH:

A pleasure.

CHARLOTTE:

Oh, how do you do! I'm Charlotte Angus. Sorry, I was busy in the kitchen when you . . . you must be Beth. So wonderful you could come! And you're Samuel. Larry's been telling me about you . . .

LARRY:

Let me introduce Garth and Marcia McCord. You already know Sam, and this is Beth Prior, just off the plane from England. I should explain that Beth and I were once, well this was years ago, but at one time . . . oh, and this is Charlotte Angus. You've met Garth, but not Marcia . . . Marcia's from New York.

MARCIA:

Actually I'm from Richmond, Virginia, but I lived in New York once, for a little over a year. Eighteen months, as a matter of fact, or maybe it was seventeen. That's probably why you thought . . .

GARTH:
How about a drink, Larry?

LARRY:
I was just about to ask.

MARCIA:
I love New York, but these days I love it tragically.

BETH:
Love it how?

CHARLOTTE:
I'll give you a hand with the champagne.

MIDGE:
Champagne? Ian, we came to the right place.

IAN:
And at just the right time.

MIDGE:
I'm Larry's sister, Midge . . . this is Ian . . . Beth and Charlotte I know, you must be Garth and Marcia . . .

SAM:
And I, lovely lady, am Samuel Diego Alvero from Seville.

MIDGE:
I'm sure you are.

LARRY:
Here's the champagne.

GARTH:
Time for a toast.

MARCIA:
Are we missing anyone?

LARRY:
Dorrie.

DORRIE:
Hello, Larry.

LARRY:
It's wonderful to see you.

DORRIE:
But it feels so strange somehow. I don't know why.

LARRY:
You're looking great.

DORRIE:
So are you.

LARRY:
Older, anyway . . . I'm almost fifty.

DORRIE:
I know. August 17th.

LARRY:
I still have the card you sent me on my fortieth.

DORRIE:
You do? I guess we should join the others.

LARRY:
Dorrie, there's something I should tell you.

DORRIE:
Yes?

LARRY:
Beth's here. Visiting from England.

DORRIE:
Beth. Oh.

LARRY:
I hope this isn't going to be awkward.

DORRIE:
Not awkward at all, Larry. Heavens, no.

LARRY:
This is Dorrie Shaw-Weller. Let me introduce you . . .
Garth and Marcia.

GARTH:
How do you do.

MARCIA:
Love your earrings. I once had a pair exactly like them
except in silver, and maybe just a little bit smaller,
and . . .

LARRY:

And this is Samuel Alvero, who's been working with me on a new maze.

SAM:

So you are a Weller also? Part of the family. This is enchanting! A family party!

DORRIE:

It's very nice to meet you, Samuel.

LARRY:

And please meet a good friend of mine, Charlotte Angus.

DORRIE:

How do you do, Charlotte.

CHARLOTTE:

We're so pleased you're here in Toronto.

LARRY:

And this is Beth Prior.

BETH:

Well, well. So you're Dorrie.

DORRIE:

So you're Beth.

BETH:

This is incredible.

DORRIE:
Isn't it? That we're meeting each other at last.

BETH:
Do you mind, Dorrie, if I give you a big hug?

GARTH:
A toast, everyone . . . to the opening of the McCord Maze.

ALL:
The McCord Maze.

GARTH:
It's a goddamn masterpiece, Larry . . . but it's more than just a maze. Because, you see, in the centre, you encounter yourself. There's a new beginning, and then you come alive again.

CHARLOTTE:
Can anyone really get lost in a maze?

DORRIE:
Larry did. At Hampton Court. On our honeymoon.

LARRY:
I wasn't really lost. I just *wanted* to be lost.

GARTH:
I think the best part of a maze is that there can be one route, or many. It means we have a choice.

SAM:
We can begin our lives again?

LARRY:
If we want to.

MIDGE:
No wonder you like mazes, baby brother.

IAN:
It's a second chance.

CHARLOTTE (*a toast*):
To all the things we could have done . . .

LARRY (*raises glass*):
Would have done.

DORRIE (*raises glass*):
Should have done.

CHARLOTTE:
Dinner is served.

LARRY:
    Look around the room,
    look at all the people.

(*Throughout the following sequence people keep saying things which trigger LARRY back to the past, and the music that plays underneath echoes these memories of people and events from years ago.*)

MARCIA:
I thought I smelled lamb when I came in!

CHARLOTTE:
Served with little white French . . .

MIDGE (*as music plays "Dot's Amazing Beans"*):
. . . beans! My God, all the years we grew up there was never a bean in our house. Our mother had a thing about them. Do you remember, Larry? Well, now I'm an adult, and I guess I could eat my fill of them . . . except I've got to watch my weight.

LARRY:
> People that I know,
> people that I knew.

BETH:
Don't be silly, Midge! You look wonderful, and so does this lamb. Larry, darling, keep it coming! I'll take that extra . . . (*as music plays "Happy Enough"*) . . . slice of lamb, and maybe a few carrots. I'm not interested in being perfect any more, I'm just interested in being. Larry, why do you keep looking at me in that strange way?

LARRY:
> Some of them I loved,
> some have even loved me.

MARCIA:
Poor Larry! You were just staring into space like your life was passing before your eyes. I know the feeling . . .

IAN:

Oh come on Marcia, give him a break. (*As music plays "Ashes to Ashes"*) I think he's doing pretty good for a guy who just sat down to dinner with his current lady friend . . . plus two ex-wives.

LARRY:

>Some are here to stay,
>some are passing through.

MARCIA:

Look, Ian you think I don't know that I talk too much? And that I say nothing? We'll get home tonight, as usual, and Garth will sit me down, and . . . (*as music plays "Round and Round Again"*) . . . we'll discuss it calmly, and once again he'll tell me what a fool I made of myself, and of him . . .

LARRY:

>But they all
>are the pieces of my life,
>from the past,
>from today.

DORRIE:

Then why do you stay with her?

GARTH:

I love her, you see . . . and I still believe that she can change. (*As music plays "Maker of Mazes"*) That we can make our lives turn out the way we hoped they would, the way we dreamed they would back when it all began . . .

LARRY:

Every one
of the pieces of my life,
takes me home,
home to stay.

DORRIE:

Did you mean what you said at the table tonight? That you weren't really lost that time we were in Hampton Court?

LARRY:

Not exactly. I was lost, but I wanted to be lost.

DORRIE:

Why didn't you tell me?

LARRY:

I wasn't sure you'd understand.

DORRIE:

I would've understood. But I wouldn't have known where to start . . . *(As music plays "What I Believe")* . . . or how to tell you that I understood.

LARRY:

Was that our problem? That we didn't know enough words?

DORRIE:

Or what we were allowed to say.

LARRY:
We could have said anything. We should have learned.

DORRIE:
Tell me, Larry, do you still want to be lost?

LARRY:
No, not any more. I want . . .

DORRIE:
What?

LARRY:
To get myself . . . found

> Look around the past,
> look around the table . . .

SAM:
What happened to your husband? Your . . .

CHARLOTTE:
. . . Derek. He died some time ago. Cancer.

SAM:
My wife, she has been dead one year. It was a depression. She took some sleeping pills. That was all *(as music plays "Little Lost Lives")*.

CHARLOTTE:
On a Sunday night when I was asleep, my Derek did the same thing as your wife. Sleeping pills. An overdose.

SAM:
Perhaps an accident . . .

CHARLOTTE:
He left a note.

SAM:
But did you not say it was cancer . . . ?

CHARLOTTE:
He was doing fine. But he was too mad at the world.
Or maybe at me.

LARRY:
> I have seen it all.
> I've been here before

CHARLOTTE:
I haven't said anything to Larry. I don't want him to
know.

SAM:
He will not hear it from me. Dear lady . . . *(as music
plays "Find the Way")*. I feel we have both been hurt the
same way. We understand each other. Perhaps, when
I leave this evening, it might be best for you to come
along with me . . .

ALL:
> Come along with me,
> come along with me,
> come along with me,
> come along with me . . .

(The singing becomes a deafening cacophony, When it reaches its peak, it suddenly cuts off, and LARRY stands alone.)

LARRY:
>   Look around the room,
>   look at all the people.
>   People that I know,
>   people that I knew.
>
>   Some of them I loved,
>   some have even loved me.
>   Some are here to stay,
>   some are passing through.
>
>   But they all
>   are the pieces of my life,
>   from the past,
>   from today.
>   Every one
>   of the pieces of my life,
>   takes me home,
>   home to stay.
>
>   Look around the past,
>   look around the table.
>   I have seen it all.
>   I've been here before
>
>   Every one I touched,
>   every one who touched me
>   took a little less,
>   gave a little more.

And they all
are the pieces of my life,
great and small
old and new.
Every one
of the pieces of my life,
brings me back,
back to you.

All the times,
I stood alone here,
on my own here
like before.
All the years
I kept on going,
never knowing
what's in store.
I have learned
to count the cost,
and I know that I'm not lost
any more,
not any more . . .

Pieces of my life,
putting them together.
Seeing how they fit,
pulling them apart.

Everything is here,
here to be discovered.
Secrets of the soul,
reasons of the heart.

I am held
in the arms of so much love,
by my son,
by my wife.
Now at last
I begin to understand
all the pieces,
the pieces of my life.

All the pieces,
the pieces of my life.

GARTH:

Garth here. Sunday afternoon. Sorry to miss you, but I'll leave a message. Great party. Marcia slept right through the night. First time in ages. Great sign. She says don't worry about her. Thanks from me too . . .

CHARLOTTE, MIDGE AND BETH:

We will go round and round again,
telling the tale of yesterday.
Starting to feel we found again
all that we lost along the way.

ALL SEVEN:

If we can look at what we were,
maybe we'll learn what we could be.

(AND LARRY):

As you go round and round
and round again with me.

LARRY *(alone)*:

Watching where we're going,
wondering where we've gone.
Half of life is knowing,
the rest is moving on.

After all the racing,
funny, but it's true.
Through the nights and the days,
at the end of the maze
is you . . .

CHARLOTTE:

I had to go into the office this morning, so I thought
I'd just slip this note under your door. I feel rotten
that I didn't stick around to help clean up last night,
but when Sam offered to drive me home, I couldn't
resist. Great party, by the way. We did it . . . whatever
"it" is.

MIDGE:

Hi, baby brother, it's just Midge here, pouring my
scattered thoughts into your voice mail. Thanks for
the great party. . . . You know, I always wondered
what would happen if you and Dorrie got together
again. I had a hunch she was waiting for a second
ride on the merry-go-round, even if she didn't know
it herself . . .

BETH:

Dear Larry, I always knew you loved her. And that
she loved you. All you needed to do was take the

right turn at the right time . . . just like one of your beautiful mazes.

ALL *(but LARRY)*:
>After all the racing,
>funny, but it's true.
>Through the nights and the days,
>at the end of the maze
>is you.

LARRY:
>Through the twisting
>and the turning
>finally learning
>where to go.
>
>Past the terror
>and the doubting
>till I'm shouting
>what I know.
>
>There's a place
>where I'm protected,
>there's a spot
>where I can stay.
>I'm prepared to take that chance, sir,
>I believe I know the answer.
>I have found the way,
>I have found the way!

BETH AND CHARLOTTE AND HERSCH:
>We will go round and round and round . . .

MIDGE AND DOT AND STU (*overlapping*):
> We will go round and round and round . . .

DORRIE AND RYAN (*overlapping*):
> We will go round and round again . . .

(DORRIE and RYAN join LARRY as they all start to exit together. Then LARRY pauses, and looks at us one last time.)

LARRY:
> Welcome to Larry's Party,
> I'm so glad you're here . . .

(End of PLAY)

FOUR SONGS

SELECTIONS FROM THE MUSICAL,

LARRY'S PARTY

(based on the novel by Carol Shields)

BOOK AND LYRICS: RICHARD OUZOUNIAN   **MUSIC: MAREK NORMAN**

1. PIECES OF MY LIFE

2. LOOK AT THE SKY

3. PART OF ME

4. ASHES TO ASHES

PIECES OF MY LIFE

[from the musical, LARRY'S PARTY]

LYRICS: RICHARD OUZOUNIAN   MUSIC: MAREK NORMAN

ALLEGRO NON TROPPO (♩=104 m.m.)

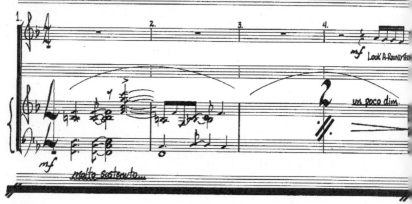

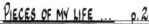

p.5 .... PIECES OF MY LIFE

10/25/00 - MN

(piano/vocal) PIECES OF MY LIFE (from the musical, LARRY'S PARTY)

LYRICS: RICHARD OUZOUNIAN   MUSIC: MAREK NORMAN

LOOK AT THE SKY

(from the musical, LARRY'S PARTY)

LYRICS: RICHARD OUZOUNIAN   **MUSIC: MAREK NORMAN**

ADAGIO CON MOTO (♩=69 m.m.)

molto legato (et sostenuto)...

SOLO MAN:

Look at the sky. ___   I thought ___ I knew ___ it so well. ___

A Tempo (dolce)

Look at the sky ___ Look-ing at me ___ Walk-ing a-way. ___

Could-n't I try, ___ Could-n't I see, ___ Could-n't I stay?

Won-der-ing when, ___ Won-der-ing how ___ And why. ___

(piano / vocal) **LOOK AT THE SKY** (from the musical, LARRY'S PARTY)

LYRICS: RICHARD OUZOUNIAN   MUSIC: MAREK NORMAN

PART OF ME

[from the musical, LARRY'S PARTY]

LYRICS: RICHARD OUZOUNIAN   MUSIC: MAREK NORMAN

I'M A PART OF YOU NOW,   You're A PART OF ME.

Pie-ces of A Puz-zle   NO ONE ELSE CAN SEE.   Pe-tals of A Flow-er,

... PART OF ME

Lyrics:

I'M A PART OF YOU NOW, YOU'RE A PART OF ME.

Un poco cresc.

THERE'S A

20 ARIOSO

THREAD THAT TIES A FATHER TO HIS SON... STRONG AS STEEL, THIN AS AIR.

AND I KNOW THAT NOW YOUR LIFE HAS JUST BE-GUN...

morendo...

IN MY

(a tempo)
... dim.   (un poco rall.)   28 MOLTO DELICATO ...

26. ARMS,   IN MY CARE.   PE-TALS OF A FLO-WER,

un poco rall.   (a tempo)

29. RIP-PLES ON A STREAM.   30. SHA-DOWS IN THE TWI-LIGHT,   31. VOI-CES IN A DREAM.

cresc.

32. PIE-CES OF A PUZ-ZLE   33. NO ONE ELSE CAN SEE.   34. I'M A PART OF YOU NOW,

(piano/vocal) **PART OF ME** (from the musical, LARRY'S PARTY)

LYRICS: RICHARD OUZOUNIAN   MUSIC: MAREK NORMAN

ASHES TO ASHES

[...from the musical, LARRY'S PARTY]

LYRICS: RICHARD OUZOUNIAN   MUSIC: MAREK NORMAN

42 **TEMPO PRIMA**

43.   *Rall.*   44.

Rall.

molto legato (et sost.)...

11/07/00 - MN

(piano / vocal) **ASHES TO ASHES** (from the musical, **LARRY'S PARTY**)

LYRICS: RICHARD OUZOUNIAN   MUSIC: MAREK NORMAN